THE BIBLE
and the
PUBLIC
SCHOOLS

A LIBERAL PRESS BOOK

Edited and with a Commentary
by
ARTHUR FROMMER

LIBERAL PRESS BOOKS
are published
by
THE FROMMER / PASMANTIER PUBLISHING CORPORATION
and are distributed
by
Affiliated Publishers
a division of POCKET BOOKS, INC.
630 Fifth Avenue
New York 20, New York

Manufactured in the United States of America

THIS BOOK has been compiled in the week following the Supreme Court decision of June 17, 1963, which forbade—as unconstitutional—the practice of devotional Bible-reading in the public schools.

That decision is set forth in full, without deletions of any kind, in the pages that follow.

The impulse to publish this book stems from our belief that Americans are entitled to read for themselves the full text of a Court document that has so materially affected their ideas of public education and caused so great a controversy. Too often in America, the opinions of Supreme Court Justices are accessible only to lawyers, or to those fortunate citizens who subscribe to the handful of newspapers that provide such texts. But even the *New York Times* failed to reprint the entire text of the Bible-reading opinions—including, in particular, the important 77-page concurring opinion of Mr. Justice Brennan.

That lack has been remedied in this book. But it provides more than that. In addition to printing the Court's decision, we have included in these pages a number of other texts—readings that deal not only with the question of religion in the public schools, but with the entire relationship of church and state in America.

This additional information has been provided in order to serve yet a second purpose—that of placing the reader in the very same position as that of a Supreme Court justice confronted with the necessity of deciding the Bible-reading question.

Law, after all, is too important a thing to be left only to judges. Every responsible citizen will want to form his own conclusions on the constitutionality of Bible-reading—and he is uniquely qualified to do so. For the briefs and oral arguments that were presented to the Court did not deal with legal issues alone, or even predominantly. Their focus was on theories of political philosophy; and they discussed such matters as the historical events that led to the enactment of the First Amendment, and the recent factual and very human controversies out of which the lawsuit over Bible-reading emerged.

For that reason, we have prefaced the Supreme Court opinion with such items as the most important writings of Jefferson and Madison on church-state issues; the debates in Congress on the formulation of the First Amendment; the stands taken by our early Presidents on the proclamation of religious ceremonies; a review of the 19th Century controversy over Catholic opposition to Bible-reading in the public schools; and finally, excerpts from the testimony in the trial of one of the very cases that was ruled upon by the Supreme Court in its June 17, 1963, decision.

All of this material has been interspersed with a commentary by the editor of this book. And therefore, the reader is entitled to know something about the bias of the editor in the church-state field.

Our bias, quite frankly, is this:

We believe that the Supreme Court's decision in the Bible-reading cases is one of the great landmarks in the history of religious freedom; that it deserves not to be castigated but to be celebrated in the same manner that Americans celebrate and revere the efforts of Jefferson and Madison that led to the enactment of the First Amendment to the Constitution of the United States.

We believe that the decision is beneficial to both the church and the state, and that any contrary result would ultimately have led to conflicts and controversies of enormous harm to the interests of religion in the United States.

But these, of course, are questions that, in the last analysis, the reader should decide for himself. In presenting the materials that follow, our primary aim is to provide the foundation upon which such a decision can wisely be based.

I
THE BIRTH OF THE UNIQUE AMERICAN PRINCIPLE THAT CHURCH AND STATE ARE TO BE SEPARATED

There are two ways to approach the interpretation of a Constitutional principle: first, by studying the history of that principle; second, by studying the modern problems to which the principle must be applied.

In the first half of this book, we shall deal with the historical background of the First Amendment; in the second half, with the modern relevance that the First Amendment has today.

The history, first. To know why the Founders of our country insisted so urgently upon a separation between church and state, one must first know something about the immediate past that shaped their views. Above all, it needs to be recalled that the men who wrote our Constitution lived at a time when the memory of religious persecutions, endorsed and fomented by the State, was still painfully fresh in their minds. As Justice Black once described it, in a Supreme Court opinion rendered in 1947:

The centuries immediately before and contemporaneous with the colonization of America had been filled with turmoil, civil strife, and persecution, generated in large part by established sects determined to maintain their absolute political and religious supremacy. With the power of government supporting them, at various times and places,

Catholics had persecuted Protestants, Protestants had persecuted Catholics, Protestant sects had persecuted other Protestant sects, Catholics of one shade of belief had persecuted Catholics of another shade of belief, and all of these had from time to time persecuted Jews. In efforts to force loyalty to whatever religious group happened to be on top and in league with the government of a particular time and place, men and women had been fined, cast in jail, cruelly tortured, and killed. Among the offenses for which these punishments had been inflicted were such things as speaking disrespectfully of the views of ministers of government-established churches, non-attendance at those churches, expressions of non-belief in their doctrines, and failure to pay taxes and tithes to support them.

It should also be remembered that these practices had not ceased with the colonization of America. For the most part, the early colonists had continued to enforce the most rigid conformity of religious belief among their members. The severity and prevalence of religious oppression had driven many of our greatest political thinkers to a state of desperation; had caused some to cry out, as James Madison did in a letter to William Bradford in 1774:

That diabolical, hell-conceived principle of persecution rages among [us]. . . . There are at this time in the adjacent county not less than five or six well-meaning men in close jail for publishing their religious sentiments, which in the main are very orthodox. I have neither patience to hear, talk, or think of anything relative to this matter; for I have squabbled and scolded, abused and ridiculed, so long about it to little purpose, that I am without common patience. So I must beg you to pity me, and pray for liberty of conscience to all.

From this sense of anguish, there developed and emerged a fiercely-held belief: that religion and the state must be entirely divorced, that each was to occupy its own independent sphere, and that neither the State was to concern itself with questions of religion, nor religion to occupy itself with matters of State.

(a) The creed of Roger Williams.

The first stirrings of this principle had long ante-dated Madison. They were the creation of the great founder of Rhode Island and religious libertarian, Roger Williams, who lived more than a hundred years before either Jefferson or Madison.

In1644, Williams had published an extraordinary pamphlet, "The Bloudy Tenent of Persecution," in which he set forth twelve reasons for the then-novel theory that society should tolerate all forms of religious opinion. In it, he first advanced the even more-novel doctrine that religious tolerance was required of the state, because of an essential difference between the nature of religion and civil government.

Here, now, are the twelve principles of Williams' classic statement; the reader should pay particular note to the fifth and tenth principles, which contain the germ of what later became America's most unique contribution to the philosophy of freedom.

THE BLOUDY TENENT OF PERSECUTION
by Roger Williams (1644)
Summary of Argument

First, that the blood of so many hundred thousand souls of Protestants and Papists, spilt in the Wars of present and former Ages, for their respective Consciences, is not required nor accepted by Jesus Christ and the Prince of Peace.

Secondly, Pregnant Scriptures and Arguments are throughout the Work proposed against the Doctrine of persecution for cause of Conscience.

Thirdly, Satisfactory Answers are given to Scriptures and objections produced by Mr. Calvin, Beza, Mr. Cotton, and the Ministers of the New England Churches and others former and later, tending to prove the Doctrine of persecution for cause of Conscience.

Fourthly, the Doctrine of persecution for cause of Conscience, is proved guilty of all the blood of the Souls crying for vengeance under the Altar.

Fifthly, All Civil States with their Officers of justice in their respective constitutions and administrations are proved essentially Civil, and therefore not Judges, Governors or Defenders of the Spiritual or Christian State and Worship.

Sixthly, It is the will and command of God, that (since the coming of his Son the Lord Jesus) a permission of the Most Paganish, Jewish, Turkish, or Anti-christian consciences and worships, be granted to all men in all Nations and Countries: and they are only to be fought against with that Sword which is only (in Soul matters) able to conquer, to wit, the Sword of God's spirit, the Word of God.

Seventhly, The state of the Land of Israel, the Kings and people therefore, in Peace and War, is proved figurative and ceremonial, and no pattern nor precedent for any Kingdom or civil state in the world to follow.

Eighthly, God requireth not an uniformity of Religion to be inacted and inforced in any civil state; which inforced authority (sooner or later) is the greatest occasion of civil War, ravishing of conscience, persecution of Christ Jesus in his servants, and of the hypocrisy and destruction of millions of souls.

Ninthly, In holding an inforced uniformity of Religion in a civil state, we must necessarily disclaim our desires and hopes of the Jews' conversion to Christ.

Tenthly, an inforced uniformity of Religion throughout a Nation or civil state, confounds the Civil and Religious, denies the principles of Christianity and civility, and that Jesus Christ is come in the Flesh.

Eleventhly, The permission of other consciences and worships than a state professeth, only can (according to God) procure a firm and lasting peace, (good assurance being taken according to the wisdom of the civil state for uniformity of civil obedience from all sorts).

Twelfthly, lastly, True civility and Christianity may both flourish in a state or Kingdom, not withstanding the permission of divers and contrary consciences, either of Jew or Gentile.

(b) The Memorial and Remonstrance of James Madison

Nearly one hundred and fifty years later, the principle suggested by Roger Williams emerged full-blown in a document that provides the clearest indication we have of the goals which the Founding Fathers sought to achieve by enacting the First Amendment.

This document was the "Memorial and Remonstrance Against Religious Assessments" by James Madison—who later led the fight for the enactment of the First Amendment and is thought to have drafted its language. Every major commentator has noted that in the "Memorial and Remonstrance" and the First Amendment, Madison sought to achieve a single consistent end—and it is therefore a text that deserves to be carefully read by every American.

The background of the "Remonstrance" is a dramatic one, that can only be hinted at in this brief summary. It involved figures famous in our history—Thomas Jefferson, George Washington, Patrick Henry, James Madison, George Mason—who were then both the political leaders of the Colony of Virginia and the most impressive panoply of public figures that any State of America has gathered together at one time.

Beginning in 1776, with the enactment of the Virginia Bill of Rights, these men had all been involved in a fierce struggle to disestablish the Anglican Church as the State church of Virginia. A wide variety of religious sects—Baptists, Lutherans, Presbyterians —had joined in this effort, and by 1784, the most oppressive religious laws of Virginia had been repealed.

Many church leaders, however, had cooperated in this movement only because they were certain that they could enact laws in Virginia which would grant state aid to *all* Christian religions, on an impartial basis.

This effort to create a "multiple" church establishment in Virginia

—that is, a system for state support of all religious sects—reached its culmination in 1784, when church leaders proposed to the Virginia legislature a "Bill Establishing a Provision for Teachers of the Christian Religion." It provided, in the words of Patrick Henry, that all citizens of Virginia would henceforth "pay a moderate tax or contribution annually for the support of the Christian religion, or of some Christian church, denomination or communion of Christians, or for some form of Christian worship." Each taxpayer would have the privilege of designating which particular Christian sect would receive his share of the tax monies. The asserted basis for the bill, as stated in its preamble, was that "the general diffusion of Christian knowledge hath a natural tendency to correct the morals of men, restrain their vices, and preserve the peace of society."

There are several crucial features of this bill which should be kept in mind—because they bear importantly on the church-state controversy which came before our own Supreme Court in 1963.

Primarily, it should be noted that the Assessment bill sought, in effect, to give aid to *all* religions, on an impartial basis. For, to all intents and purposes, the various denominations of the Christian religion were the only religions then extant in Virginia. One commentator, Leo Pfeffer, has pointed to the fact that there were at that time no more than half a dozen Jews in the entire colony. Moreover, the bill had been interpreted by George Washington to permit persons to "declare themselves Jews, Mohametans, or otherwise," and thereby gain an exemption from its provisions.

Thus, the issue was squarely posed: ought the state to grant aid to all forms of religion, across the board? Having abolished the single establishment of the Anglican church, could the state substitute a "multiple establishment" of all churches?

To this, James Madison responded with a resounding "No." "Religion," he said, "is wholly exempt from the cognizance of Civil society."

We now set forth, in pertinent part, James Madison's famous "Memorial and Remonstrance."

A MEMORIAL AND REMONSTRANCE AGAINST RELIGIOUS ASSESSMENTS
by James Madison (1784)

To the Honorable the General Assembly of the State of Virginia.

We, the subscribers, citizens of the said commonwealth, having taken into serious consideration a bill printed by order of the last session of the general assembly, entitled "A bill for establishing a provision for teachers of the Christian religion," and conceiving that the same, if finally armed with the sanctions of a law, will be a dangerous abuse of power, are bound, as faithful members of a free state, to remonstrate against the said bill—

(1) Because we hold it for a "fundamental and undeniable truth," that religion, or the duty which we owe to our creator, and the manner of discharging it, can be directed only by reason and conviction, not by force or violence. The religion, then, of every man, must be left to the conviction and conscience of every man; and it is the right of every man to exercise it as these may dictate. This right is, in its nature, an unalienable right. It is unalienable, because the opinions of men, depending only on the evidence contemplated in their own minds, cannot follow the dictates of other men; it is unalienable, also, because what is here a right towards men, is a duty towards the creator. It is the duty of every man to render the creator such homage, and such only, as he believes to be acceptable to him; this duty is precedent, both in order of time and degree of obligation, to the claims of civil society. . . . We maintain, therefore, that in matters of religion no man's right is abridged by the institution of civil society; and that religion is wholly exempt from its cognizance. True it is, that no other rule exists, by which any question which may divide society can be ultimately determined, but the will of the majority; but it is also true, that the majority may trespass on the rights of the minority.

(2) Because, if religion be exempt from the authority of the society at large, still less can it be subject to that of the legislative body. The latter are but the creatures and vicegerents of the Former. Their jurisdiction is both derivative and limited. It is limited with regard to the coordinate departments; more necessarily is it limited with regard to the constituents. The preservation of a free government requires not merely that the metes and bounds which separate each department of power be universally maintained; but more especially, that neither of them be suffered to overleap the great barrier which defends the rights of the people. The rulers who are guilty of such an encroachment, exceed the commission from which they derive their authority, and are tyrants. The people who submit to it are governed by laws made neither by themselves, nor by an authority derived from them, and are slaves.

(3) Because it is proper to take alarm at the first experiment on our liberties. We hold this prudent jealousy to be the first duty of citizens, and one of the noblest characteristics of the late revolution. The freemen of America did not wait till usurped power had strengthened itself by exercise, and entangled the question in precedents. They saw all the consequences by denying the principle. We revere this lesson too much soon to forget it. Who does not see that the same authority which can establish Christianity, in exclusion of all other religions, may establish, with the same ease, any particular sect of Christians, in exclusion of all other sects? That the same authority that can call for each citizen to contribute three pence only of his property for the support of only one establishment, may force him to conform to any one establishment, in all cases whatsoever?

(4) Because the bill violates that equality which ought to be the basis of every law, and which is more indispensable in proportion as the validity or expediency of any law is more liable to be impeached. If "all men by nature are equally free and independent," all men are to be considered as entering into society on equal conditions, as relinquishing no more, and therefore, retaining no less, one than another, of their rights. Above all, they are to be considered as retaining an "equal right to the free exercise of religion, according to the dictates of conscience." While we assert for ourselves a freedom to embrace, to profess, and to observe, the religion which we believe to be of divine origin, we cannot deny an equal freedom to those whose minds have not yet yielded to the evidence which has convinced us. If this freedom be abused, it is an offence against God, not against man: to God, therefore, not to man, must an account of it be rendered. As the bill violates equality by subjecting some to peculiar burdens, so it violates the same principle by granting to others peculiar exemptions. Are the Quakers and Menonists the only sects who think compulsive support of their religions unnecessary and unwarrantable? Can their piety alone be entrusted with the care of public worship? Ought their religions to be endowed, above all others, with extraordinary privileges, by which proselytes may be enticed from all others? We think too favorably of the justice and good sense of these denominations to believe that they either covet preeminence over their fellow citizens, or that they will be seduced by them from the common opposition to the measure.

(5) Because the bill implies, either that the civil magistrate is a competent judge of truth, or that he may employ religion as an engine of civil policy. The first is an arrogant pretension, falsified by the contradictory opinions of rulers in all ages, and throughout the world: the second is an unhallowed perversion of the means of salvation.

(6) Because the establishment proposed by the bill is not requisite for the support of the Christian religion. To say that it is, is a contradiction to the Christian religion itself; for every page of it disavows a dependence on the powers of this world: it is a contradiction to fact; for it is known that this religion both existed and flourished, not only without the support of human laws, but in spite of every opposition from them; and not only during the period of miraculous aid, but long after it had been left to its own evidence and the ordinary care of Providence. Nay, it is a contradiction in terms; for a religion not invented by human policy must have pre-existed and been supported before it was established by human policy. It is, moreover, to weaken in those who profess this religion a pious confidence in its innate excellence, and the patronage of its author; and to foster in those who still reject it, a suspicion that its friends are too conscious of its fallacies to trust it to its own merits.

(7) Because experience witnesseth that ecclesiastical establishments, instead of maintaining the purity and efficacy of religion, have had a contrary operation. During almost fifteen centuries has the legal establishment of Christianity been on trial. What have been its fruits?

More or less, in all places, pride and indolence in the clergy; ignorance and servility in the laity; in both, superstition, bigotry, and persecution. Enquire of the teachers of Christianity for the ages in which it appeared in its greatest lustre; those of every sect point to the ages prior to its incorporation with civil policy. Propose a restoration of this primitive state, in which its teachers depended on the voluntary rewards of their flocks; many of them predict its downfall. On which side ought their testimony to have the greatest weight, when for, or when against, their interest?

(8) Because the establishment in question is not necessary for the support of civil government. If it be urged as necessary for the support of civil government only as it is a means of supporting religion, and if it be not necessary for the latter purpose, it cannot be necessary for the former. If religion be not within the cognizance of civil government, how can its legal establishment be said to be necessary to civil government? What influences, in fact, have ecclesiastical establishments had on civil society? In some instances they have been seen to erect a spiritual tyranny on the ruins of civil authority; in many instances they have been seen upholding the thrones of political tyranny; in no instance have they been seen the guardians of the liberties of the people. Rulers who wished to subvert the public liberty may have found an established clergy convenient auxiliaries. A just government, instituted to secure and perpetuate it, needs them not. Such government will be best supported by protecting every citizen in the enjoyment of his religion with the same equal hand that protects his person and property; by neither invading the equal rights of any sect, nor suffering any sect to invade those of another.

(9) Because the proposed establishment is a departure from that generous policy which, offering an asylum to the persecuted and oppressed of every nation and religion, promised a lustre to our country, and an accession to the number of its citizens. What a melancholy mark is the bill, of sudden degeneracy. Instead of holding forth an asylum to the persecuted, it is itself a signal of persecution. It degrades from the equal rank of citizens all those whose opinions in religion do not bend to those of the legislative authority. Distant as it may be, in its present form, from the inquisition, it differs only in degree. The one is the first step, the other the last, in the career of intolerance. The magnanimous sufferer under this cruel scourge in foreign regions, must view the bill as a beacon on our coast, warning him to seek some other haven, where liberty and philanthropy, in their due extent, may offer a more certain repose from his troubles.

(10) Because it will have a like tendency to banish our citizens. The allurements presented by other situations are every day thinning their numbers. To superadd a fresh motive to emigration, by revoking the liberty which they now enjoy, would be the same species of folly which has dishonored and depopulated flourishing kingdoms.

(11) Because it will destroy the moderation and harmony which the

forbearance of our laws to intermeddle with religion has produced among its several sects. Torrents of blood have been spilt in the world in vain attempts of the secular arm to extinguish religious discord, by proscribing all differences in religious opinions. Time, at length, has revealed the true remedy. Every relaxation of narrow and rigorous policy, wherever it has been tried, has been found to assuage the disease. The American theatre has exhibited proofs, that equal and complete liberty, if it does not wholly eradicate it, sufficiently destroys its malignant influence on the health and prosperity of the state. If, with the salutary effects of this system under our own eyes, we begin to contract the bounds of religious freedom, we know no name that will too severely reproach our folly. At least, let warning be taken at the first fruits of the threatened innovation. The very appearance of the bill has transformed that "Christian forbearance, love, and charity," which of late mutually prevailed, into animosities and jealousies, which may not soon be appeased. What mischiefs may not be dreaded, should this enemy to the public quiet be armed with the force of a law.

(12) Because the policy of the bill is adverse to the diffusion of the light of Christianity. The first wish of those who enjoy this precious gift ought to be, that it may be imparted to the whole race of mankind. Compare the number of those who have as yet received it, with the number still remaining under the dominion of false religions, and how small is the former! Does the policy of the bill tend to lessen the disproportion? No: it at once discourages those who are strangers to the light of revelation from coming into the region of it; countenances, by example, the nations who continue in darkness, in shutting out those who might convey it to them. Instead of levelling, as far as possible, every obstacle to the victorious progress of truth, the bill, with an ignoble and un-Christian timidity, would circumscribe it with a wall of defence against the encroachments of error.

(13) Because attempts to enforce by legal sanctions acts obnoxious to so great a proportion of citizens, tend to enervate the laws in general, and to slacken the bands of society. If it be difficult to execute any law which is not generally deemed necessary or salutary, what must be the case where it is deemed invalid and dangerous? And what may be the effect of so striking an example of impotency in the government on its general authority?

(14) Because a measure of such general magnitude and delicacy ought not to be imposed, without the clearest evidence that it is called for by a majority of citizens: and no satisfactory method is yet proposed, by which the voice of the majority in this case may be determined, or its influence secured. "The people of the respective counties are, indeed, requested to signify their opinion, respecting the adoption of the bill, to the next sessions of assembly"; but the representation must be made equal before the voice either of the representatives or the counties will be that of the people. Our hope is, that neither of the former will, after due consideration, espouse the dangerous prin-

ciple of the bill. Should the event disappoint us, it will still leave us in full confidence that a fair appeal to the latter will reverse the sentence against our liberties.

(15) Because, finally, "the equal right of every citizen to the free exercise of his religion, according to the dictates of his conscience," is held by the same tenure with all our other rights. If we recur to its origin, it is equally the gift of nature; if we weigh its importance, it cannot be less dear to us; if we consult the "declaration of those rights which pertain to the good people of Virginia, as the basis and foundation of government," it is enumerated with equal solemnity, or, rather, studied emphasis.

Either, then, we must say that the will of the legislature is the only measure of their authority, and that, in the plenitude of this authority, they may sweep away all our fundamental rights; or, that they are bound to leave this particular right untouched and sacred: either we must say that they may control the freedom of the press, may abolish the trial by jury, may swallow up the executive and judiciary powers of the state; nay, that they may despoil us of our right of suffrage, and erect themselves into an independent and hereditary assembly: or, we must say, that they have no authority to enact into law the bill under consideration.

We, the subscribers, say, that the General Assembly of this commonwealth have no such authority; and that no effort may be omitted, on our part, against so dangerous an usurpation, we oppose to it in this Remonstrance—earnestly praying, as we are in duty bound, that the Supreme Lawgiver of the Universe, by illuminating those to whom it is addressed, may, on the one hand, turn their councils from every act which affronts His holy prerogative, or violates the trust committed to them; and, on the other, guide them into every measure that may be worthy of His blessing, may redound to their own praise, and may establish more firmly the liberties of the people, and the prosperity and happiness of the commonwealth.

The Remonstrance succeeded. The legislation that sought to create a "multiple establishment" of religion in Virginia, was defeated.

And then, having turned back this attempt to unite church and state, Madison moved to the attack, by proposing legislation in Virginia that would *affirmatively* forbid such "establishment" for all time.

(c) The Statute of Religious Freedom
The weapon he used was the soaring prose of his colleague, Thomas Jefferson, who had drafted a proposed "Statute for Establishing Religious Freedom in Virginia," the key declaration of which was the statement "that to compel a man to furnish contributions

of money for the propagation of opinions which he disbelieves, is sinful and tyrannical."

That statement necessarily meant that government could at no time grant aid to either one religion, some religions, or all religions —for even a non-believer was protected from having his taxes go to the support of religion. Indeed, in his Autobiography, Jefferson wrote that his great Statute for Religious Freedom had "meant to comprehend, within the mantle of its protection, the Jew and the Gentile, the Christian and the Mohometan, the Hindoo, and Infidel of every denomination."

The Statute of Religious Freedom was enacted into law in Virginia in 1786. We now reprint it in full:

AN ACT FOR ESTABLISHING RELIGIOUS FREEDOM
by Thomas Jefferson (1786)

Well aware that Almighty God hath created the mind free; that all attempts to influence it by temporal punishments or burdens, or by civil incapacitations, tend only to beget habits of hypocrisy and meanness, and are a departure from the plan of the Holy Author of our religion, who being Lord both of body and mind, yet chose not to propagate it by coercions on either, as was in his Almighty power to do;

That the impious presumption of legislators and rulers, civil as well as ecclesiastical, who, being themselves but fallible and uninspired men, have assumed dominion over the faith of others, setting up their own opinions and modes of thinking as the only true and infallible, and as such endeavoring to impose them on others, hath established and maintained false religions over the greatest part of the world, and through all time;

That to compel a man to furnish contributions of money for the propagation of opinions which he disbelieves, is sinful and tyrannical; that even the forcing him to support this or that teacher of his own religious persuasion, is depriving him of the comfortable liberty of giving his contributions to the particular pastor whose morals he would make his pattern, and whose power he feels most persuasive to righteousness, and is withdrawing from the ministry those temporal rewards, which proceeding from an approbation of their personal conduct, are an additional incitement to earnest and unremitting labors for the instruction of mankind;

That our civil rights have no dependence on our religious opinions, more than our opinions in physics or geometry; that, therefore, the proscribing any citizen as unworthy the public confidence by laying upon him an incapacity of being called to the offices of trust and emolument, unless he profess or renounce this or that religious opinion, is depriving him injuriously of those privileges and advantages to which in common with his fellow citizens he has a natural right;

That it tends also to corrupt the principles of that very religion it is meant to encourage, by bribing, with a monopoly of worldly honors and emoluments, those who will externally profess and conform to it; that though indeed these are criminal who do not withstand such temptation, yet neither are those innocent who lay the bait in their way;

That to suffer the civil magistrate to intrude his powers into the field of opinion and to restrain the profession or propagation of principles, on the supposition of their ill tendency, is a dangerous fallacy, which at once destroys all religious liberty, because he being of course judge of that tendency, will make his opinions the rule of judgment, and approve or condemn the sentiments of others only as they shall square with or differ from his own;

That it is time enough for the rightful purposes of civil government, for its officers to interefere when principles break out into overt acts against peace and good order;

And finally, that truth is great and will prevail if left to herself, that she is the proper and sufficient antagonist to error, and has nothing to fear from the conflict, unless by human interposition disarmed of her natural weapons, free argument and debate, errors ceasing to be dangerous when it is permitted freely to contradict them.

Be it therefore enacted by the General Assembly, That no man shall be compelled to frequent or support any religious worship, place or ministry whatsoever, nor shall be enforced, restrained, molested, or burthened in his body or goods, nor shall otherwise suffer on account of his religious opinions or belief; but that all men shall be free to profess, and by argument to maintain, their opinions in matters of religion, and that the same shall in nowise diminish, enlarge, or affect their civil capacities.

And though we well know this Assembly, elected by the people for the ordinary purposes of legislation only, have no power to restrain the acts of succeeding assemblies, constituted with the powers equal to our own, and that therefore to declare this act irrevocable, would be of no effect in law, yet we are free to declare, and do declare, that the rights hereby asserted are of the natural rights of mankind, and that if any act shall be hereafter passed to repeal the present or to narrow its operation, such act will be an infringement of natural right.

In the years of his retirement, Thomas Jefferson wrote that there were three accomplishments for which he wished to be remembered: the Declaration of Independence, the founding of the University of Virginia—and the Virginia Statute of Religious Freedom.

(d) The First Amendment

The fight for church-state separation, which Madison and Jefferson led and won in Virginia, set the stage and created the influences that resulted, within five years, in the enactment of the Bill of Rights, whose *first sentence,* in the First Amendment, reads: "Congress shall make no law respecting an establishment of religion or prohibiting the free exercise thereof . . ." Madison was the sponsor of the Amendment and the leading member of the committee which drafted its provisions.

The record of the Congressional debates on the phrasing of the First Amendment, make it clear that Congress sought to achieve the very ends that Madison and Jefferson had earlier sought in their Virginia struggles. Time and again, efforts were made to limit the language of the First Amendment so that it would prevent no more than the giving of preferential aid to a particular religious sect; and on each such occasion, the effort failed.

Thus, in the Senate, a motion was made to replace the words "Congress shall make no law respecting an establishment of religion" with the words:

"Congress shall make no law respecting an establishment of one religious sect or society in preference to others."

The motion was defeated.

A motion was then made to substitute the words:

"Congress shall not make any law infringing the rights of conscience, or establishing any religious sect or society."

It, too, was defeated.

A motion was then made to substitute the language:

"Congress shall make no law establishing any particular denomination of religion in preference to another. . . ."

And this, also, was defeated. The amendment passed in its full sweep: "Congress shall make no law respecting an establishment of religion or prohibiting the free exercise thereof. . . ."

With respect to this legislative history, Bishop Anson Phelps Stokes has written:

This action was significant in showing that Congress was not satisfied with a proposal which merely prevented an advantage to any one denomination over others as far as Church-State separation was concerned. It wished to go further.

(e) The dissenting view

In spite of this—and despite numerous Supreme Court decisions to the contrary—a body of thought has continued to flourish in the nation that the purpose of the Establishment Clause of the First Amendment was a narrow one, which did not proscribe the granting of impartial aid to all religions, but merely forbade aid to a particular sect or sects.

Can any fair-minded citizen who has read Madison's Remonstrance, or Jefferson's Statute, give serious credence to that interpretation?

For Madison, the man who sponsored the First Amendment, was the same man who, in his Remonstrance, had specifically opposed the granting of government aid to all religions, had proclaimed that "religion is wholly exempt from the cognizance of Civil society," had warned that government may not "employ religion as an engine of civil policy," and that the support of religion is "not necessary for the support of civil government."

Madison was the same man who, in point 9 of his Remonstrance (see above), had referred to an assessment bill for the benefit of *all* religions, as an "Establishment."

And the man who first called attention to the need for a Bill of Rights—Thomas Jefferson—was the same man who, in one of the three proudest acts of his life, had stated that it was "sinful and tyrannical" to force any man to contribute a single penny to the support of religious beliefs with which he disagreed.

Clearly, they believed with a firmness approaching passion, that religion was to occupy a wholly different sphere from that of government; that each had its functions and these functions were different; and that to keep these functions separate was in the best interests of religion and in the best interests of the State.

(e) The later acts of Jefferson and Madison

If there were any doubt about the accuracy of this assessment of church-state beliefs on the part of the Founding Fathers, it was dispelled by their later actions in office.

Thomas Jefferson refused, as President, to issue proclamations of Thanksgiving and fasts, so strongly did he feel the need to keep church and state separate.

In 1804, he refused to declare a fast day because, he said, he feared to "disturb the security which religion now enjoys in this country, in its complete separation from the political concerns of the General Government."

Similarly, James Madison, following his Presidency, expressed himself as strongly opposed to such proclamations; and years later, Andrew Jackson issued an identical refusal to proclaim a day of fasting, on grounds of church-state separation.

Again, then, these men proved by their own acts that the First Amendment was intended to have the most far-reaching consequences.

In fact, it was in direct connection with a refusal to proclaim a religious holiday that Jefferson first used the metaphor of "a Wall" to describe the separation that had taken place in America between Church and State. When, in 1802, the members of the Danbury Baptist Association petitioned Jefferson to proclaim a day of fasting in commemoration of the Revolutionary War, Jefferson responded with the following address:

ADDRESS TO THE DANBURY BAPTISTS
by Thomas Jefferson (1802)

To Nehemiah Dodge, Ephraim Robbins, and Stephen S. Nelson: A Committee of the Danbury Baptist Association, Connecticut, January 1, 1802.

The affectionate sentiments of esteem and approbation which you are so good as to express towards me, on behalf of the Danbury Baptist Association, give me the highest satisfaction.

My duties dictate a faithful and zealous pursuit of the interests of my constituents, and in proportion as they are persuaded of my fidelity to those duties, the discharge of them becomes more and more pleasing.

Believing with you that religion is a matter which lies solely between man and his God, that he owes account to none other for his faith or his worship, that the legislative powers of government reach actions only, and not opinions, I contemplate with sovereign reverence that act of the whole American people which declared that their legislature should "make no law respecting an establishment of religion, or prohibiting the free exercise thereof," thus building a wall of separation between Church and State. Adhering to this expression of the supreme will of the nation in behalf of the rights of conscience, I shall see with sincere satisfaction the progress of those sentiments which tend to restore to man all his natural rights, convinced he has no natural right in opposition to his social duties.

I reciprocate your kind prayers for the protection and blessing of the common Father and Creator of man, and tender you for yourselves and your religious association, assurances of my high respect and esteem.

Proponents of the narrow construction of the First Amendment have been quick to argue that Jefferson's "wall of separation" was an offhand phrase, that was most likely scribbled in a hasty and unconsidered manner.

Unfortunately for them, recent historical discoveries have proven that Jefferson gave the most careful thought to his Danbury Baptists address, and regarded it as an important state document. It has been learned, in fact, that on the morning of the day that he sent off his address, Jefferson first sent a copy to his Attorney-General,

Levi Lincoln, for the latter's comments and suggestions. Jefferson wrote as follows:

LETTER TO LEVI LINCOLN
by Thomas Jefferson (January 1, 1802)

Averse to receiving addresses, yet unable to prevent them, I have generally endeavored to turn them to some account, by making them the occasion, by way of answer, of sowing useful truths and principles among the people, which might germinate and become rooted among their political tenets. The Baptist address, now enclosed, admits of a condemnation of the alliance between Church and State, under the authority of the Constitution. It furnishes an occasion, too, which I have long wished to find, of saying why I do not proclaim fastings and thanksgivings, as my predecessors did. The address, to be sure, does not point at this, and its introduction is awkward. But I foresee no opportunity of doing it more pertinently. I know it will give great offence to the New England clergy; but the advocate of religious freedom is to expect neither peace nor forgiveness from them. Will you be so good as to examine the answer, and suggest any alternations which might prevent an ill effect, or promote a good one, among the people? You understand the temper of those in the North, and can weaken it, therefore, to their stomachs; it is at present seasoned to the Southern taste only. I would ask the favor of you to return it, with the address, in the course of the day or evening.

Plainly, then, Jefferson was indulging in no mere rhetoric when he trumpeted forth his belief in "a Wall of Separation between Church and State."

As for James Madison, so fierce was his continuing devotion to the separation principle that he took the extreme position of urging members of Congress to themselves contribute money for the support of Congressional chaplains, and to prohibit the payment of these chaplains' salaries from public funds.

In his most famous utterance on the subject, Madison wrote:

THE DETACHED MEMORANDA
of James Madison

Is the appointment of Chaplains to the two Houses of Congress consistent with the Constitution, and with the pure principle of religious freedom?

In strictness the answer on both points must be in the negative. The Constitution of the United States forbids everything like an establishment of a national religion. The law appointing Chaplains establishes a religious worship for the national representatives, to be performed by ministers of religion, elected by a majority of them; and these are to be paid out of national taxes. Does not this involve the principle of a national establishment applicable to a provision for a religious worship for the Constituent as well as of the Representative Body, approved by the majority and conducted by ministers of religion paid by the entire nation?

The establishment of the Chaplainship to Congress is a palpable violation of equal rights as well as of Constitutional principles. The tenets of the Chaplains elected shut the door of worship against the members whose creeds and consciences forbid a participation in that of the majority. To say nothing of other sects, this is the case with that of Roman Catholics and Quakers who have always had members in one or both of the Legislative branches. Could a Catholic clergyman ever hope to be appointed a Chaplain? To say that his religious principles are obnoxious or that his sect is small is to lift the veil at once and exhibit in its naked deformity the doctrine that religious truth is to be tested by numbers, or that the major sects have a right to govern the minor.

If Religion consists in voluntary acts of individuals, singly or voluntarily associated, and if it be proper that public functionaries, as well as their own constituents, should discharge their religious duties, let them, like their constituents, do so at their own expense. How small a contribution from each member of Congress would suffice for the purpose!

Better also to disarm in the same way the precedent of Chaplainships for the army and navy, than erect them into a political authority in matters of Religion. The object of this establishment is seducing; the motive to it is laudable. But is it not safer to adhere to a right principle, and trust to its consequences, than confide in the reasoning, however specious, in favor of a wrong one?

And in a letter written to Edward Livingstone in the twilight of his life, on July 10, 1822, Madison summarized his views:

I observe with particular pleasure the view you have taken of the immunity of Religion from civil jurisdiction, in every case where it does not trespass on private rights or the public peace. This has always been a favorite principle with me; and it was not with my approbation that the deviation from it took place in Congress, when they appointed Chaplains, to be paid from the National Treasury. It would have been a much better proof to their constituents of their pious feeling if the members had contributed for the purpose a pittance from their own pockets. As the precedent is not likely to be rescinded, the best that can now be done, may be to apply to the Constitution the maxim of the law, de minimis non curat.

Naturally, one need not agree with Madison's views on the appointment of chaplains, to agree with his broader philosophy on the strict separation of church and state—or on the application of these principles to the public schools. As Senator Hart of Michigan stated in the 1962 Senate hearings on questions of church and state:

I have always felt that it is this matter of compulsion that is the basis for the distinction. There is a real difference between a 10-year-old in a classroom listening to a teacher reciting a prayer, and a 30- or 40- or 50- or 60-year-old Senator who may or may not do his best on the Senate floor at noon.

But Madison's views on Congressional chaplains are nevertheless important, if only because they again reveal his fierce adherence to the separation of church and state, which he believed was absolutely necessary for the preservation of liberty in the United States.

This, too, was the belief of Thomas Jefferson. And together, these two patriots created a barrier against government involvement in matters of religion that has lasted for over 175 years, and that constitutes what is probably America's most unique contribution to the philosophy of freedom. Virtually alone among the nations of the world, the United States permits no establishment of either multiple sects or a single sect.

Who can deny that this policy—considering the nature of our country—is the only one that could insure religious tranquility? It has permitted 180,000,000 persons of the most amazing diversity of religious opinion and belief to live together in harmony. It has avoided the bitter religious conflicts witnessed in other nations. As James Bryce wrote in his classic work, "The American Commonwealth":

Half the wars of Europe, half the internal troubles that have vexed European states, from the Monophysite controversies in the Roman Empire of the fifth century down to the Kulturkampf in the German empire of the nineteenth, have arisen from theological differences or from the rival claims of church and state. This whole vast chapter of debate and strife has been avoided in the U.S.

And finally, this separation between matters of church and state has, we submit, effectively guaranteed an almost absolute freedom of religious thought, which is one of the great glories of our nation.

II
THE EMERGENCE OF A FREE AND SECULAR PUBLIC SCHOOL SYSTEM

In the years that followed enactment of the First Amendment, the American people began to move towards yet another political development of momentous importance: the creation of a system of free public schools.

Today we take this phenomenon for granted. But at the time of its development, the public school was a unique and unprecedented institution. Side by side with the American principle of separation between church and state, it constitutes one of the two great contributions that America has made to the structuring of democracy.

For certainly, few would deny that, in its largest aspect, the public school system has been an unparalleled success. It has helped to forge a democratic, harmonious nation out of persons with incredibly diverse backgrounds and beliefs. In the words of Conrad Moehlman, a Professor Emeritus of the History of Christianity at Colgate-Rochester Divinity School:

All groups in the United States have always met and mingled in public schools. They thus became the spiritual clearing house of American ideas. In spite of all religious hatred, the common school wrought a miracle. The youthful representatives of the various races and creeds and nations sat side by side in the same classrooms, at first blissfully ignorant of the antagonistic views of their elders.

But the public school did not spring out of a vacuum. It existed, and flourished, only because the American people grew steadily more convinced, in the years that followed adoption of the First Amendment, that the separation of church and state was absolutely necessary to the workings of our democracy. Without that belief, the public school system—with all the benefits it has brought us— could never have existed.

This interrelationship between the separation principle and the public school system, was described by Justice Felix Frankfurter in a classic opinion written by him in the famous McCollum case in 1948. It charts the development of American attitudes towards the public schools as follows:

FROM THE CONCURRING OPINION OF JUSTICE FELIX FRANKFURTER IN ILLINOIS EX REL. MC COLLUM

Traditionally, organized education in the Western world was church education . . . [And] the emigrants who came to these shores brought this view of education with them. Colonial schools certainly started with a religious orientation.

The evolution of [this system of] colonial education, largely in the service of religion, into the public school system of today, is the story of changing conceptions regarding the American democratic society, of the functions of State-maintained education in such a society, and of the role therein of the free exercise of religion by the people. The modern public school derived from a philosophy of freedom reflected in the First Amendment. It is appropriate to recall that the Remonstrance of James Madison, an event basic in the history of religious liberty, was called forth by a proposal which involved support to religious education.

As the momentum for popular education increased and in turn evoked strong claims for state support of religious education, contests not unlike that which in Virginia had produced Madison's Remonstrance appeared in various forms in other states. New York and Massachusetts provide famous chapters in the history that established dissociation of religious teaching from State-maintained schools. In New York, the rise of the common schools led, despite fierce sectarian opposition, to the barring of tax funds to church schools, and later to any school in which sectarian doctrine was taught. In Massachusetts, largely through the efforts of Horace Mann, all sectarian teachings were barred from the common school to save it from being rent by denominational conflict.

The upshot of these controversies, often long and fierce, is fairly summarized by saying that long before the Fourteenth Amendment subjected the states to new limitations, the prohibition of furtherance by the state of religious instruction became the guiding principle, in law and feeling, of the American people. In sustaining Stephen Girard's will, this Court referred to the inevitable conflicts engendered by matters "connected with religious polity" and particularly "in a country composed of such a variety of religious sects as our country." Vidal et al. v. Girard's Executors, 2 How. 127, 198, 11 L. Ed. 205. That was more than one hundred years ago.

Separation in the field of education, then, was not imposed upon unwilling states by force or superior law. In this respect the Fourteenth Amendment merely reflected a principle then dominant in our national life. To the extent that the Constitution thus made it binding upon the states, the basis of the restriction is the whole experience of our people. Zealous watchfulness against fusion of secular and religious activities by Government itself, through any of its instruments but especially through its educational agencies, was the democratic response of the American community to the particular needs of a young and growing nation, unique in the composition of its people.

It is pertinent to remind that the establishment of this principle of separation in the field of education was not due to any decline in the religious beliefs of the people. Horace Mann was a devout Christian, and the deep religious feeling of James Madison is stamped upon the Remonstrance. The secular public school did not imply indifference to the basic role of religion in the life of the people, nor rejection of religious education as a means of fostering it. The claims of religion were not minimized by refusing to make the public schools agencies for their assertion. The non-sectarian or secular public school was the means of reconciling freedom in general with religious freedom. The sharp confinement of the public schools to secular education was a recognition of the need of a democratic society to educate its children, insofar as the state undertook to do so, in an atmosphere free from pressures in a realm in which pressures are most resisted and where conflicts are most easily and most bitterly engendered.

Designed to serve as perhaps the most powerful agency for promoting cohesion among a heterogeneous democratic people, the public school must keep scrupulously free from entanglement in the strife of sects. The preservation of the community from divisive conflicts, of Government from irreconcilable pressures by religious groups, of religion from censorship and coercion however subtly exercised, requires strict confinement of the state to instruction other than religious, leaving to the individual's church and home, indoctrination in the faith of his choice.

(a) *The struggle to keep religious practices from the public schools.*

At the conclusion of the words quoted above, Mr. Justice Frankfurter remarked that:

This development of the public school as a symbol of our secular unity was not a sudden achievement nor attained without violent conflict.

And with these words, we are introduced to the conflict that has raged for more than a hundred years in America over whether the Bible may be read as a devotional exercise in the public schools—a conflict that reached at least a temporary culmination in the Supreme Court decision of June 17, 1963.

Few Americans are aware that the struggle over Bible-reading has had so long a history. But in reality, at least a dozen state courts have been confronted with this question in the last century, and have given varying rulings, some prohibiting the practice, others permitting it.

Even fewer Americans are aware that in the late 1800's, the chief leadership in the fight against Bible-reading in the public schools was provided—to its everlasting credit—by the Catholic Church. So fierce was this opposition, in fact, that many scholars have attributed the triumph of secular public education in the United States to the battle that was waged in the 1800's by leading Catholic Bishops and priests against devotional religious exercises in the schoolroom.

It is both instructive and thought-provoking to study the history of Catholic opposition to Bible-reading in the public schools in the 1800's. That stand was of course based, in great part, upon the well-known antipathy of the Church to the King James translation of the Bible. The preface to the King James Bible, which even today continues to appear in many editions of it, states with utter baldness that the purpose of the translation was to give "such a blow unto that Man of Sin (the Pope) as will not be healed."

In 1843, the Catholic Bishop of Philadelphia petitioned the school board of that city to permit Catholic children to use the Douay version of the Bible in the daily Bible-reading exercises then required in the Philadelphia schools.

Philadelphia was, at the time, the center of the anti-Catholic "Nativist" movement. The reaction of the "Nativists" to this protest against the "Protestant Bible" set off one of the most infamous chapters in American history—the "Nativist riots." They are described as follows by Leo Pfeffer, in his book, "Church, State and Freedom":

The immediate effects of the Bishop's petition were both dramatic and tragic. For several months the controversy simmered, and then suddenly erupted in riots. Catholic churches were attacked; two churches in the Philadelphia suburb of Kensington were reduced to ashes. A convent was completely destroyed. Bishop Kenrick ordered all Catholic worship suspended and every Catholic church in the city closed; but this action did not avert the more serious consequences that the

Bishop hoped it would. Many houses in the Irish section were destroyed by fire, some of the residents were shot down as they ran out, and a number of non-Catholic bystanders likewise lost their lives.

Throughout the country, in the years that followed, the Bible controversy continued to rage, causing incidents of religious persecution—directed against Catholic opponents of Bible-reading—that are shocking in the extreme. They are movingly described by Pfeffer in the following scenes:

In 1854 a Jesuit priest, John Bapst, formerly President of Holy Cross College, was engaged in missionary work among the Indians in Maine. Among the parishes he served was the town of Ellsworth, near Bangor. The school committee of the town adopted a regulation requiring all children to read the King James Bible. Father Bapst advised his parishoners to defy the committee and take the issue to the courts for judicial determination. Acting on his urging, the father of Bridget Donahoe directed his daughter to refuse to read from the Protestant Bible as directed by her teacher. When the rebellious Bridget was expelled, her father brought suit to compel her reinstatement.

Father Bapst's action became known to the residents of the town, who indignantly called a town meeting, at which a resolution was adopted to the effect that if Father Bapst ever entered Ellsworth again he would be tarred and feathered and ridden out of town on a rail. A few months later Father Bapst returned to Ellsworth, and while hearing confessions on Saturday night, a mob broke into his house, dragged him out, tore off his clothing, tarred and feathered him, and after two hours of cruel treatment, finally released him. Although the ringleaders were known and the grand jury was in session, no one was indicted or even arrested in connection with the incident.

* * *

Five years later a Massachusetts court was faced with a problem arising from the stubborn rebellion of another Catholic child. Tom Wall was an eleven-year-old pupil in a Boston public school where the Bible was read daily and the Ten Commandments recited weekly. The evidence showed that Tom's "father had told him for his life not to say them [the Commandments], and that his priest had also told him not to say them, and that on the Sunday previous to March 14th, the priest [Father Wiget] while addressing nine hundred children of St. Mary's Church, of whom Wall was one, told them not to be cowards to their religion, and not to read or repeat the Commandments in school, and that if they did he would read their names from the altar."

The next day Tom Wall came to school, "with the determination not to read or repeat" the Commandments. (For this, it appears, he later

received a blessed medal from Father Wiget.) Moreover, some sixty others of his Catholic schoolmates, comprising about two-thirds of the children of the school, likewise announced that they would not repeat the Commandments. Here was rebellion on a large scale, and it was clear to McLaurin F. Cooke, the teacher, that Tom Wall was the ring-leader. With the approval of the principal, the teacher urged Tom to obey, "but Wall, still refusing, was punished . . . with a rattan stick, some three feet in length and three-eighths of an inch thick, by whip-ping upon his hands. From the time the punishment commenced to the time when it ended, repeated inquiries were made of Wall if he would comply with the requirements of the school. Some thirty minutes time was occupied in the whole," but the conclusion was obvious from the beginning. Eleven-year-old Tom Wall could hardly hold out forever against the majesty and power of the Commonwealth of Massachusetts. After thirty minutes of chastisement "Wall submitted to the require-ment of the school," and the "master ceased to punish."

* * *

It should not be supposed that the cases of Bridget Donahoe and Tom Wall were unique. About the same time that Tom Wall was flogged for his rebellious refusal to participate in reading from the Protestant Bible, some one hundred other Catholic children were expelled for the same reason. In Indiana in the 1880's a Catholic girl who refused to learn a chapter from the Protestant Bible as required, recited "Maud Muller" instead. Here again was rebellion, but this time the rod was spared; instead the child was kept after school day after day in an attempt to break her stubborn will. Apparently only physical force is adequate to break religious conscience, for unlike Tom Wall the Indiana girl never did yield.

Lawsuits by Catholic plaintiffs, challenging the reading of the Bible in the public schools, were brought throughout the nation—mostly to no avail.

But by 1870, the first glimmer of a counterreaction had set in, led by citizens who once again studied the doctrines of Jefferson and Madison and came to appreciate the need for once again proclaim-ing the separation of church and state.

In Cincinnati, Ohio, the local school board itself repealed the practice of requiring Bible-reading in the public schools. And after a fierce litigation in the courts, its right to do so was upheld by the Ohio Supreme Court, which ruled that there could be no connection between the state and religion. It wrote:

Legal Christianity is a solecism, a contradiction of terms. When Chris-tianity asks the aid of government beyond mere impartial protection, it denies itself. Its laws are divine, and not human. Its essential inter-ests lie beyond the reach and range of human governments. United

with government, religion never rises above the merest superstition; united with religion, government never rises above the merest despotism; and all history shows us that the more widely and completely they are separated, the better it is for both.

(b) The present-day attitudes

Today, the official policy of the Catholic Church in America has apparently reversed itself on the Bible-reading issue. On the day following the Supreme Court decision of June 17, 1963, three of the five Roman Catholic Cardinals from the United States issued statements that bitterly attacked the Court's ruling. Cardinal Cushing called it "a great outrage." Cardinal Spellman stated that "no one who believes in God, and I say believes in God, can approve such a decision." Cardinal McIntyre asserted that the ruling "can only mean that our American heritage of philosophy, of religion and of freedom, are being abandoned in imitation of Soviet philosophy, of Soviet materialism and of Soviet-regimented liberty."

No mention was made by either of the three Cardinals of the past Church opposition to Bible reading and of the stands taken in the 1800's by Bishop Kenrick, by Bishop Hughes of New York, or by the Jesuit priests who underwent physical violence in opposing the requirement that the King James Bible be read in the public schools.

Among Catholic laymen, however, there remains a residue of concern about the consequences of the fusion of religious practices with public school education. No one has expressed this concern more cogently—or more effectively—than the present-day Senator from Michigan, Senator Hart—a Catholic.

The occasion for Senator Hart's statement were the hearings held before the Senate Committee on the Judiciary in July of 1962, following the Supreme Court's decision in the case of *Engel* v. *Vitale,* which forbade the recitation of a State-composed prayer in the public schools. That decision came down almost precisely a year before the Supreme Court's ruling on Bible-reading, and it provoked a storm of Congressional protest.

Three Constitution amendments were presented to the Senate, modifying the Bill of Rights to permit prayer reading in the public schools. Senator after senator spoke out in favor of these amendments and in condemnation of the Supreme Court. Scarcely a single dissenting voice was heard. A real possibility existed that the 87th Congress might tamper with the work of Jefferson and Madison.

It was at this point in July of 1962 that Senator Hart spoke out, introducing doubts that seem to have checked the momentum of these efforts, in an almost conclusive way.

The transcript of this portion of the Senate hearings runs as follows:

SENATOR HART. I think in fairness I should make this comment. I agree with you, that whatever else the decision may have done, it shows that the relationship between religion and public life in this country needs a thorough reexamination. I think as a nation we appear to be pretty well muddled about the meaning of this in our contemporary society, but I think the Engel decision was completely predictable and is consistent with a long line of Federal and State decisions.

I know this runs counter to your presentation, but I was reminded of what could be described as a personal situation. You mentioned the reading of the Bible and the Lord's Prayer as something that in most American communities, I take it in the public schools, has always been thought of to be fine.

SENATOR STENNIS. Fine?

SENATOR HART. And nobody could suggest that this might not be what this society wanted nor the Constitution permitted.

But if the Bible that is read, and the Lord's Prayer that is recited, were not the Bible and the Lord's Prayer of my children, although I am a Christian—does it not really do damage to my children to be exposed to that? How do I explain to them this inconsistency? You see, I am a Catholic; our Bible and our Lord's Prayer differ from the Protestant version.

SENATOR STENNIS. Yes.

SENATOR HART. Is this an unreasonable expression of a minority to be concerned about the youth in public schools?

To this important query, it can charitably be said that the proponents of a constitutional change proceeded to flounder. Senator Stennis of Mississippi, for example, answered as follows:

SENATOR STENNIS. Well, I feel that the key to your question, Senator, is the choice that has always existed. We have done mighty well under this system. I do not know precisely how, but I do know that everyone has gotten along mighty well. When people wanted the Bible read, it has been read. Those who had other desires did not attend. Arrangements have been made for participation by Mr. X's children in one place, and for Mr. Y's children in another. Over the years it has worked out splendidly. That is a part of the American system, and when we just ban it, throw it all out and uproot it, it seems to me that we throw overboard a great deal that is basic for the spiritual training and tradition that we want to encourage in the home and, of course, in the church.

I would not make it compulsory on anyone, of course.

SENATOR HART. We encourage it in the home and in the church, and then we send them to school and they run into a 180° switch. This is a basic problem. It is one that I think that we can fruitfully examine.

SENATOR STENNIS. Well, I agree with you. You run into various angles of the problem, but I do not think that the remedy is to throw everything overboard.

Senator Hart returned to his inquiry time and again, eliciting responses from U.S. Senators that may cause some Americans to sit up in wonder:

SENATOR HART. To clarify our thinking and to assist the record, what if the prayer that was cited in the Maryland school had been the "Hail Mary?"—would not some non-atheist object to that? What would the law be on it?

SENATOR ROBERTSON. Well, I am not familiar with the "Hail Mary" or what is in it. However, I think that if it is voluntary, there might be no more objection to the "Hail Mary" than to the Lord's Prayer.

Eventually Senator Hart summarized his views, and the hearing ended with a statement of regret by the presiding senator that these disquieting questions had come up:

SENATOR HART. Thank you, Mr. Chairman. I do have one comment upon that decision of the Supreme Court. I know that it is quoted in full at the outset of this record, but I would like to ask leave to read part of one sentence from the majority opinion.

Mr. Justice Black is describing the emotions which caused Europeans to come to this country originally and he said they—" * * * came to this country filled with the hope that they could find a place in which they could pray when they pleased to the God of their faith in the language they chose."

I think that all of us want to do our utmost to make sure that is the kind of society we maintain and that when we talk about changing the First Amendment let us recognize we are talking about something that has taken us a long way for a long time and we would be wise to consider most critically any change that is proposed.

SENATOR THURMOND. Mr. Chairman, I do not know whether the Senator wants any comment or not.

SENATOR HART. No. I am sure the Senator from South Carolina agrees that that was the motivation, and that tradition ought to be preserved.

SENATOR JOHNSTON. I think we all believe in prayer when we please and to the God of our faith, and there is no question as to our rights there.

SENATOR HART. But we do not ask anybody else to join us.

SENATOR JOHNSTON. That is true. I am sorry the question has come

up and I hope that none of us gets so heated about some particular issue that we will lose our way, so to speak, and not do justice in this field.

No Congressional action has yet been taken on the Constitutional amendments offered in 1962. But hard on the heels of the Supreme Court's Bible-reading decision of June 17, 1963, still another such amendment was offered by a group of Senators, including, most prominently, Senator Goldwater of Arizona. It would revise the First Amendment to permit devotional religious practices in the public schools. Other senators, and numerous religious figures, have suggested an amendment that would go further, by permitting states to provide impartial aid to all religious groups, including, presumably, religious schools. And these proposals may very well receive serious consideration in the months and years ahead.

Certainly, therefore, every American must soon decide to what extent he is willing to revise our earlier notions of a thoroughly-secular public school system. Shall we permit religious teachings in the public schools that may be offensive to one or more groups? Shall we further the development of private religious schools by diverting a portion of tax funds to the support of such schools?

Or do we yet hold with such men as Horace Greeley, who wrote:

When the time shall come for apportioning our children to Catholic Orthodox, Liberal, Baptist, Methodist and Unitarian primary schools, I shall apprehend that the last sands of the Republic are nearly run. When our common schools shall have perished, we may still have a country; but it will not be the land of Liberty and Equality for which our fathers toiled and suffered, and poured out their blood.

or with President Grant, who in 1875 made these famous remarks to the Convention of the Army of the Tennessee:

Encourage free schools and resolve that not one dollar appropriated for their support shall be appropriated for the support of any sectarian schools. Resolve that neither the state nor the nation, nor both combined, shall support institutions of learning other than those sufficient to afford every child growing up in the land the opportunity of a good common school education, unmixed with sectarian, pagan, or atheistical dogmas. Leave the matter of religion to the family altar, the church, and the private school, supported entirely by private contributions. Keep the church and state forever separated.

III
THE PANDORA'S BOX:
A REVIEW OF SOME PROBLEMS
THAT MIGHT ARISE
IF THE SUPREME COURT
WERE TO RULE DIFFERENTLY

At this point in our discussion, it might prove illuminating if we were to pursue a hypothetical situation. Assume that the Supreme Court had ruled otherwise in its Bible-reading decision. We believe that the consequences of such an assumption are fairly staggering to contemplate.

(a) Assume, first, that the Supreme Court had ruled that government could give impartial aid to all religions.

In order to reach such a contrary verdict on the Bible-reading question, the Supreme Court would probably have had to rule that the First and Fourteenth Amendments merely forbade a state from giving preferential aid to one religious sect as against another, but did not forbid impartial aid to all religions, on an equal footing.

This is, in fact, precisely the position that has been taken by the Catholic Church, by a minority of Protestant ministers led by Bishop Pike and Billy Graham, and by most Southern senators. Earlier in this book, we have stated our own belief that this interpretation of the Constitution is historically inaccurate; but now, what of its practical difficulties?

(1) To any citizen who gives serious thought to the "impartial-aid-to-all-religions" argument, the question soon presents itself:

How? Is it realistically possible? For just as a radio station that grants free air time to the candidate of a major political party, will soon find itself besieged by demands for equal time from the candidates of the Vegetarian, Prohibition and Socialist Workers parties, will not the state that gives "impartial" aid to the major religions soon find itself saddled with undeniable requests from hundreds of minor sects?

The United States possesses countless religious movements. Would not aid have to be given to all? And on what basis? Is twice as much aid to be given to a major sect as to a minor one? Is aid to be given on a per capita basis? Does not such aid permanently maintain the superior size and influence of a major religion over a minor one?

(2) Then, too, who is to determine what groups in the United States are "religious" groups and thus entitled to government aid? Must not such a decision be made by a government official, who will thus possess life-and-death powers over the fortunes of a particular movement? Does not the power to grant aid necessarily mean the power to regulate the recipient?

Are the Black Muslims a religious movement? Is the Ethical Culture Society? Are certain Pacifist groups religious or secular in their origins? Are they to be given state aid? Is any group which claims to be a religious group to be given state aid? And if their claims of religious status are denied, is that not a denial of their religious liberty?

(3) What of the rights of non-believers, or of citizens who belong to no organized church? Are their tax monies to be used to promote religious beliefs with which they disagree? Has the United States become unsafe for irreligion? Is "heresy" to be defined by the State, and given a less preferred position than that occupied by the orthodox? Such results would certainly come as a surprise to Thomas Jefferson, who earnestly advanced the contention that in a democracy, the rights of non-believers must be zealously guarded.

(4) Finally, the advocates of the contention that the First Amendment permits impartial aid to all religions, should recognize that their theory would make constitutional the granting of public aid to parochial schools—to Jewish Yeshivas, to Catholic schools, to schools operated by the Black Muslim movement, to schools of the Jehovah's Witnesses—who are vehemently anti-Catholic—in short, to any private school operated by a religious group. Most assuredly, such aid would tend to the breakdown of the American

public schools. Is this a result sought by most Americans? Curiously enough, the proponents of a narrow construction of the First Amendment, include several Protestant leaders who vehemently oppose public aid to parochial schools—a result which their stand would most certainly bring about in many States.

(b) Assume, second, that the Supreme Court had directly ruled that Bible-reading could be made a devotional practice in the public school.

Here, any contrary ruling by the Supreme Court would surely have meant a perpetuation of practices that were unfair to numerous children of minority religious status—and of harmful value, many felt, to even those in majority groups.

The "Christian Century," a leading Protestant magazine published in Chicago, stated the case best in its October 24, 1962 issue:

If the court should decide that the reading of the Bible as a devotional exercise and the repetition of the Lord's Prayer are practices consistent with the intent of the First Amendment, tormenting and divisive questions will rise: What version of the Bible will be used—the Douay, the King James, the Revised Standard? Who will decide what ten verses should be read? The teacher? Can a public school teacher, an employee of the state, select a passage of Scripture for a public school class without violating the Constitution? Shall the children select the reading? Imaginative young people have been known to select passages of Scripture which appeal to their prurient rather than to their spiritual interests. Would not Jews demand readings from the Old Testament; Christian Scientists readings from Science and Health; Mormons, from the Book of Mormon? Which Lord's Prayer? When the Roman Catholic children complete their Pater Noster will they remain reverently quiet while the Protestant children add ". . . the kingdom and the power and the glory forever . . ."? Meanwhile, what about the Jews, the Unitarians, the atheists, the Moslems, the Hindus—have they no choice but to listen daily to Christian prayer or to suffer the embarrassment of withdrawing from the presence of their schoolmates? Why should random passages of Scripture be read to children without comment? Is the Bible a talisman, a cabalistic charm? There will be no end to such questions and no end to the controversies they will raise. It seems entirely unlikely that a Supreme Court which has repeatedly restored the wall between church and state, which has been consistently faithful to the First Amendment, will now open a Pandora's box by legalizing the use of sectarian scriptures and prayers in public schools.

The contents of the "Pandora's Box," so well summarized in the above editorial, become even more troublesome when one stops to take a closer and more searching look at them.

(1) It is impossible, first, to minimize or pass off the continuing struggle between Protestant and Catholic groups over the version of the Bible to be read. One still encounters, on the part of both groups, firm insistence on their own text. Thus, for example, a leading Catholic theologian is reported as having advised Catholic teachers in public schools to avoid using the "Protestant Bible" and instead to "bring their own Bible to class and read it to the pupils" when Bible reading was required. And similarly, the statement continues, when recitation of the Lord's Prayer is called for, neither the Catholic teacher nor Catholic pupils are to recite the phrase, "For thine is the kingdom," because "in practice these words have taken on a Protestant connotation, so their use would constitute an implicit approval of heresy."

(2) And what, indeed, of the position of Jewish children in the public schools, when devotional use of the New Testament is made? Certainly it is difficult to justify—as the advocate of Bible-reading necessarily must—that the parents of these children must pay taxes to support devotional readings of portions of the New Testament that are offensive to the Jewish religion. Moreover, it is difficult to deny that portions of the Bible—when read to children without comment or explanation—may instill deep-rooted prejudices and hates: as, for example, when a child reads, as a devotional exercise, the famous scene in Matthew 27, in which the Jews of Jerusalem are portrayed as refusing to exchange Barabbas for Jesus and demanding that the crucifixion of Jesus proceed. "Then answered all the people," says the New Testament, "His blood be on us, and our children." With respect to this passage, Rabbi Solomon Grayzel has testified that it has been the cause of more anti-Jewish riots and pogroms through the ages than any other factor.

(3) The advocates of devotional Bible-reading must face up to still another important question, and provide an answer to it: the increasing diversity of religious beliefs in America. For, if majority groups in one State can choose the Bible as a devotional text, then obviously the Buddhists of Hawaii, who constitute a majority there, can choose the holy writings of their religion for devotional use in the Hawaiian public schools. The Mormons of Utah can do the same. The Catholic majority of Rhode Island might well choose a Catholic text for the same purpose.

(4) To these vexing questions, the standard response of Bible-reading advocates has been that a child whose religious beliefs are at variance with the text that is read, can step outside the classroom, and wait in the hall, during the devotional readings.

It can hardly be argued, in our opinion, that this is a satisfactory alternative, or that it does not infringe upon the religious liberty of the non-conforming child. Those familiar with the problems faced by minority children in the public schools, know that these problems are already quite heavy. To require that the child call attention to his minority status on every day of the school year—and appear to be out of step with the moral teachings of the school authorities—would surely be to make his life unbearable. As Justice Frankfurter wrote in 1948:

That a child is offered an alternative may reduce the constraint; it does not eliminate the operation of influence by the school in matters sacred to conscience and outside the school's domain. The law of imitation operates, and non-conformity is not an outstanding characteristic of children. The result is an obvious pressure upon children to attend.

Nothing said here is inconsistent with the general and accepted rule that a non-conformer must expect embarrassment as a result of his non-conformity and be proud of it. But certainly in a democracy, and particularly in the United States, a non-conformer has the right to expect that the instruments of the State will not be used to further that embarrassment. The minority child and his parents are a part of the State, and are entitled to the guarantee that, in matters of religion, the power of their own government will not be used to their disadvantage.

(5) No citizen of the United States would regard it as constitutional if the law were to require every school child to arise in the classroom every morning and declare the religious beliefs to which he held. Such would be a compulsory profession of faith, and under our constitution, every citizen's religious beliefs are his own business and concern of no one else. Yet to require that child to leave the classroom in order to avoid participation in an offensive religious ceremony, is to require that he profess his faith in public, every day. And that, we submit, is clearly unconstitutional.

(6) Finally, it must always be recalled that the public schools are supported by taxes imposed upon every citizen. To conduct religious school ceremonies that are offensive to any class of citizens, is to compel those citizens to pay taxes for the propagation of religious

opinions with which they disagree. This is precisely the practice that Thomas Jefferson called "sinful and tyrannical" and which he sought to prohibit for all time.

Any proponent of devotional religious practices in the public schools, or of a break-down in the separation between church and state, must answer the questions and provide solutions to the problems that are posed above. We shall now proceed to examine the two lawsuits that were presented to the Supreme Court involving these questions; and the reader may then compare his own answers with the majority, concurring, and dissenting opinions of nine Justices of the Court.

IV
THE MURRAY AND THE SCHEMPP CASES

The two lawsuits that resulted in the Supreme Court's Bible-reading decision of June 17, 1963, bear ponderous titles: *William Murray, Infant, by Madalyn E. Murray, his mother and next friend, v. the Board of School Commissioners of Baltimore City;* and *School District of Abington Township, Pennsylvania v. Edward Lewis Schempp et al.*

We shall call them the Murray and the Schempp cases.

(1) In the first case, the plaintiff, Madalyn Murray, was an atheist, whose son, William, attends the public schools of Baltimore, Maryland. In Baltimore, the school board required that each school day begin with the "reading, without comment, of a chapter in the Holy Bible and/or the use of the Lord's Prayer."

Mrs. Murray refused to permit her son to participate in these exercises; and on each morning, he withdrew from the classroom and stood in the hallway outside, or in a special room, while the Bible was being read. Eventually, Mrs. Murray brought suit against the Baltimore school board, charging that the Bible-reading practices had subjeted her son to indignities and coercion, and infringed his and her religious liberty.

The facts in the Murray case were never subjected to a trial, involving testimony of witnesses—but this was no fault of Mrs. Murray's.

For, instead of challenging the allegations of her complaint, the Baltimore school board "demurred" to it—that is, it "admitted" her factual allegations for purposes of the lawsuit, but claimed that these allegations were legally insufficient to give her a basis for relief. Consequently, neither Mrs. Murray nor her son were ever given the opportunity to testify concerning their charges.

It is instructive, however, to read one of Mrs. Murray's reports about the events that transpired when she and her sons decided to challenge the Bible-reading practice. She has described these events as follows:

Bill was beaten up so badly [by other school children] and so often that he was never without multiple bruises for the entire school year. Our car was vandalized, for sums over a hundred dollars, and so was the car of my parents. . . . Our home was stoned, egg-splattered, as was our car. We were stopped in the streets to have people spit in our faces. Our cat was stolen; our flowers were trampled. We received bushel baskets of opprobrious mail with many threats. Our entire neighborhood ostracized us and my little (then six year old) son [Mrs. Murray's younger son, Garth] came often to the house weeping because the neighborhood children jeered him as an "Atheist" and refused to play with him. He begged me to explain Hell to him, where all the kids said he was going.

Certainly, such scenes should give pause to those who say that the onus is removed from devotional practices in the schools by reason of a dissenting child's right to leave the classroom. In the world of children, tolerance apparently does not result so easily.

(2) In the second case to reach the Supreme Court, the objecting parents were Unitarians, who carried on the old-fashioned practice of reading the Bible to their children at home, where they were able to explain its contents and to teach their own attitudes towards it. These were Mr. and Mrs. Edward Schempp, whose three children attend the public schools of Abington, Pennsylvania. Here, too, devotional Bible-reading began each school day, by direction of the law of the State of Pennsylvania.

The Schempps, however, refused to request that their children be excused from the morning exercises, believing that any such withdrawal would mark their children as pariahs among their classmates. Instead, the Schempps brought suit to invalidate the practice; and here, a full trial was had, at which both Mr. Schempp and his three children testified.

Portions of that testimony provide an interesting insight into the objections that religiously-minded citizens can have to compulsory Bible-reading in the schools. We shall reprint below the highlights of the trial, as presented by both the plaintiffs (the Schempps) and the defendant (the local school district).

The case for the Schempps began with the testimony of their oldest son, Ellory, 18, who had graduated from the public schools of Abington County, Pennsylvania, after attending both the elementary and high schools of that district. Excerpts from his testimony now follow:

Q. Ellory, are you, through your father, one of the plaintiffs in this case?

A. Yes, I am.

Q. What is your age?

A. Eighteen.

Q. Did you attend the Roslyn Elementary School?

A. I did.

Q. Did you attend the Abington Junior High School?

A. Yes.

Q. And did you attend the Abington Senior High School?

A. Yes.

* * *

Q. Now, Ellory, will you tell us the time, the place and the manner of that reading of the Bible, and what Bible it was up to your time, up to the 10th grade that you were in school.

A. The teacher would usually at the beginning of the year give the Bible reading over to the students, such that it was read by the students in rotation.

Q. And who selected the verses to be read?

A. The children.

Q. And what Bible, if you know, was it that was read?

A. The King James version.

Q. Now, was there a change in that practice in the 11th and 12th grades?

A. There was inasmuch as that we had a new high school and a centralized P.A. system was installed, therefore, the Bible was read over this P.A. system.

* * *

Q. By whom was the reading done over the P.A. system?

A. The P.A. system was run, shall we say, by a special class of the high school which was known as the Radio and Television Workshop. This was a regular school class and the members of this class were responsible for reading the announcements and taking care of Bible reading, etc.

Q. Now, will you describe for us precisely what happened upon your arrival in school in the morning and where you went?

A. Late bell was at 8:15; we went to our home rooms and approximately 8:20 a few opening bars of music would be played in order to gain the students' attention and following that immediately a student would announce over the P.A. system that a certain verse of the Bible was to be read. He would immediately proceed to read this verse and upon finishing he would say would the students please rise and repeat the Lord's Prayer.

* * *

Q. Now, what is this exercise known as?
A. Morning devotions.

* * *

Q. Was there ever an occasion, Ellory, when the teacher gave any directive to the class as to their deportment or conduct during the reading of the Lord's Prayer?
A. Yes, there was.
Q. And what was that directive, if any?
A. I have frequently heard teachers say to the class to be quiet or to pay attention, as the case required.
Q. And during the recitation of the Lord's Prayer was there any directive given by the teachers or any of them to the students on any occasion?
A. Not specifically, no.
Q. Now, did there come a time when you objected to the reading of the King James version of the Bible and, if so, will you tell us when it was and under what circumstances?
A. In late November of 1956, I had over a period of time been thinking about the matter and had come to feel that it had been, the compulsory reading of the King James version of the Bible was an infringement upon my right to think and believe religiously as I wanted to, and at this time I brought a copy of the Koran into class and while the Bible was being read I read this, and at the time that the rest of the students rose to repeat the Lord's Prayer, I remained seated and continued reading the Koran.

* * *

Q. Now, before we pursue what happened as a result of that, Ellory, let me ask you: What were the features of religious conscience and thought to which you objected in respect to the reading of the King James version?
A. I felt that, well, on two points. First of all, I felt that it was a clear violation of the separation of church and state, and that the Bible reading was a religious practice being condoned and forced by the state, and I objected on that point, and also on the grounds of my own personal feelings of religion. I do not believe in the Bible literally and I felt that being read as it was in class it suggested that it was to be taken literally.
Q. Well, let me ask you this at this point: What is your religious affiliation?

A. Unitarian.

* * *

Q. Mr. Schempp, do you believe in the divinity of Christ?
A. I do not.
Q. Were you read in the course of your instruction at Abington High School material from the Bible which asserted the divinity of Christ?
A. Yes, sir.
Q. Do you believe in the Immaculate Conception?
A. No.
Q. Were you read material during the course of your time at Abington High School which asserted the truth of the Immaculate Conception?
A. There was.

* * *

Q. Do you believe in God?
A. Yes.
Q. Do you believe in an anthropomorphic God?
A. No.
Q. Were you read material from the King James version during your time at Abington which asserted the truth of the concept of the Trinity?
A. I believe so.

* * *

Q. Now, what happened, Ellory, on the occasion in which you did not participate in the reading of the King James version and did not stand during the reading of the Lord's Prayer? What took place thereafter?
A. It was in late November of 1956, in the morning devotional period, I brought a copy of the Koran and read it during the Bible reading.
  By Judge Kirkpatrick:
Q. You mean you read it aloud?
A. Read it to myself. And then as the rest of the class stood up for the Lord's Prayer, I remained seated and continued reading it.
  By Mr. Sawyer:
Q. And what happened?
A. Well, soon thereafter the home room teacher came to my desk and said that hereafter I should stand for the Lord's Prayer. I replied to him that I did not feel that I could do this in keeping with my religious conscience and asked that I, or said that I, thought I should be excused from the morning devotions.

Ellory's younger sister, Donna, 12, also testified:

Q. Where do you go to school, Donna?
A. Huntington Junior High School.
Q. And how old are you?
A. I am twelve.
Q. What grade were you in last year?
A. Seventh.

Q. Did they read the Bible in the seventh grade at the Huntington Junior High School?
A. Yes, they did.
Q. When did they read it and how did they read it?
A. They read it in the morning the first thing and it was read in the beginning of the year by the students.
Q. How did the students—how did they pick what student was going to read it on any given morning?
A. Whoever volunteered.
Q. Whoever volunteered.
And who picked the passage that was to be read?
A. The student.

* * *

Q. Now, did that—well, after the Bible was read, then what happened?
A. Then we would rise for the Lord's Prayer.
Q. And would somebody tell you to rise?
A. Well, it was just done as a matter of habit.
Q. And would the Lord's Prayer then be said—who said it then, everybody or what?
A. The whole class.
Q. And what was this occasion called in the morning? What did the kids call it?
A. Morning Devotions.
Q. Did the teachers refer to it also as Morning Devotions?
A. The teachers didn't really refer to it.
Q. And did you ever—did you notice at any time that there was a change in this way of doing it, and, if so, what was it?
A. About late November or early December, the teacher suddenly decided that she was going to be the one to read it.
Q. And did she then—was she then the one to read it?
A. Yes.
Q. Well, before that what had the teacher done when it was being read?
A. She paid—she would make sure everybody was listening and then she herself would pay attention.
Q. And did you observe any difference in the deportment and attention that was required of the students during the Bible reading than would be during ordinary teaching?
A. Well, during the Bible reading everybody was supposed to make sure they were doing nothing else and that they were—their eyes were facing the person that was reading it.
Q. And was that always required when someone or the teacher was reading some other work?
A. Not necessarily.
Q. Now, do you go to Sunday school?
A. Yes, I do.
Q. Where do you go?
A. The Unitarian Church of Germantown.
Q. Did you ever have anything that was read to you in the Bible which

was different from what they taught you in Sunday school?
A. I have.
Q. Could you tell us of any of those that you can remember?
A. Well, I can think of a few. In Sunday school we have been taught that in the Bible that where it says that the devil came down to Jesus and tempted Him, we have been taught that that was just a dream. And it is a matter of fact in the Bible.
Q. And is there anything else you have heard read to you in the school-room that you don't believe in—I mean read to you from the Bible?
A. Well, we have been—well, in the Ten Commandments, where it says, "I am a jealous God," I have come to believe that if a God was ever jealous I don't see how He could be good. If that is the type of world that everybody believes in, it's pretty horrible.

And also I don't think any man would have the powers to do the miracles that the Bible says He does.
Q. When you say "man," do I take it that you don't believe that Jesus Christ was actually the son of God?
A. I do not believe that.
Q. And did you ever recall any instance where any of your school friends had any particular reaction to Bible reading? Could you tell us about that?
A. Well, I do know a Jewish friend who was listening to a part of the Bible where I think it was when Jesus washed the feet of a man and something happened—I don't exactly recall—and she got almost so fed up with it because she didn't believe in it that she was going to walk out of the room.

* * *

Q. Donna, did this friend of yours actually say anything to you about this?
A. Yes, she did.
Q. What did your friend say, Donna?
A. She said that she was just plain fed up.

Substantially similar testimony was given by the Schempp's third child, Roger, 15.

The father of the Schempp children, Edward Lewis Schempp, also took the stand to outline his position, testifying in part:

Q. What are the grounds for your objection to this practice, Mr. Schempp?
A. The Bible reading in the school, is given by the manner of presentation, the ten verses without comment, is given a degree of authority or devotion or religious significance above normal school authority, in my opinion; and then under that particular atmosphere, statements are read from the Bible, from the literal Bible, with which I do not agree.

Q. But what would be such statements? Give some examples of statements in the Bible with which you do not agree.

A. Well, we have Leviticus where they mention all sorts of blood sacrifices, uncleanness and leprosy. Nobody believes in these things today, yet they are in the Bible. And in some parts, some of the lower grades, the children are allowed to select verses and they could just as well pick verses from Leviticus. I don't believe that they would be picked by an adult.

The Old Testament has Jehovah as a God of vengeance. We have—there is a verse sandwiched right in between the Ten Commandments in which "God will visit the sins upon the fourth generation." That has been read in Abington High School.

A human father would not visit the sins upon the children of a fourth generation, in my opinion. That makes God less than man and I do not want my children believing that God is a lesser person than a human father. My concept of God is bigger than that.

We have parts—another part that says something like, "The animal that dies of itself—" or "The meat that dies of itself thou shalt not eat," but then "Thou mayest feed it to the stranger within thy gates." That's nothing—that's quite foreign to my concept of being good and religious and moral. There's many things like that.

Q. And do you attend any church with your children, Mr. Schempp?

A. We attend regularly the Unitarian Church of Germantown.

When asked to state why he had not availed himself of the right to have his children excused from the Bible-reading exercises, Mr. Schempp testified as follows:

Q. Were you aware of the provision which enabled you to have your children excused from the Bible reading ceremony?

A. I am aware of that.

Q. Did you consider whether or not you would elect to utilize that provision with respect to your two children?

A. We considered it very seriously.

Q. What conclusion did you come to?

A. We decided the children would stay in class.

Q. Mr. Schempp, what reasons entered into your decision with respect to deciding not to ask for your children to be excused from the Bible reading ceremony?

A. We originally objected to our children being exposed to the reading of the King James version of the Bible, which we felt was against our particular family religious beliefs, and under those conditions we would have theoretically liked to have had the children excused. But we felt that the penalty of having our children labelled as "odd balls" before their teachers and classmates every day in the year was even less satisfactory than the other problem.

There were a number of things that we considered at the time.

The children, the classmates of Roger and Donna, are very liable to label and lump all particular religious difference or religious objections as atheism, particularly, today the word "atheism" is so often tied to astheistic communism, and atheism has very bad connotations in the minds of children and many adults today. They consider Johnny as an atheist, therefore, he is un-American, he is anti-Red, he is immoral and other things.

* * *

Q. Mr. Schempp, were there any other reasons or considerations which impelled your decision which you have told us about?

A. There are the mechanics of being excused in school. . . . The children report at 8:15; just a minute or two afterwards the Bible reading begins with the children seated at attention. Then they stand and the Lord's Prayer—

By Judge Biggs:

Q. Did you say the children seated at attention?

A. During the Bible reading, yes, which is over the P.A. system at this particular time. Then the children stand and with the P.A. system leading them, they repeat the Lord's Prayer; with no gap, still standing, they then give the flag salute, then they sit down and the announcements, which are very important to a child, immediately follow this. There is no gap in between where the child might come in or go out of the class without considerable trouble or time involved. And we felt that these, any—

Q. When you say "we"—speak for yourself. You felt.

A. I felt, that's right, my wife and myself felt, in considering it with my oldest son Ellory and my other children, that the experimenting that would be required to make these excuses from school would be very detrimental to the psychological well-being of our children.

This is the mechanical part of it we are objecting to.

* * *

Q. Mr. Schempp, are you familiar with any various modes of punishment which may from time to time be used in the Abington High School?

A. In Abington and in other schools which our children have attended in Abington High School, one of the penalties, common penalty, is that bad boys stand in the hall during classes. We felt that this was a reason to be considered, that they would have the stigma of being— this is a form of punishment.

The Schempps produced one expert witness to testify on their behalf—Dr. Solomon Grayzel, Editor-in-Chief of the Jewish Publication Society and a Biblical scholar. Dr. Grayzel testified as to various differences between Jewish and Christian attitudes towards portions of the Bible, and of the problems encountered by Jewish children in a predominantly Christian society. Portions of his testimony follow:

Q. Now, Dr. Grayzell, are there any books—first of all, is there any general section of the King James version of the Bible which is not to be found in the Jewish Holy Scripture?

A. Our sacred books consist of the three divisions which—we divide the Bible into three parts, the Torah, which is the five books of Moses, the prophetic portion from, I mean the historical books and the Prophets from Joshua down to the end of the prophetic tradition Malachi, and then the sacred writings, including everything else, the Psalms, the Proverbs and all the others down through Chronicles, which differs considerably from the Christian tradition in the order of the books and in the contents of the Bible.

Q. In the view of the Jewish church, do all of the books have equal importance and weight from the standpoint of their religious value?

A. There is a distinction which every Jew makes. The highest sanctity is ascribed to the five books of Moses.

By Mr. Rhoads:

Q. That is the Torah?

A. The Torah. Lesser, somewhat lesser sanctity is ascribed to the historical and the prophetic books, and least sanctity, though sacred too, naturally, is ascribed to the so-called sacred writings, Psalms and the rest.

May I add this: That in the King James version, of course, the order of the books is completely different, I mean from a Christian viewpoint understanding, and, besides, there is added the New Testament, which the Jewish Bible naturally does not have at all.

By Mr. Sawyer:

Q. Now, the Jewish Bible, in other words, does not contain the New Testament?

A. No.

* * *

Q. What is the position, the doctrine of the Jewish religion with regard to the New Testament, specifically with regard to the figure known as Jesus Christ?

A. The Jews have, naturally, not believing in the divinity of Jesus, have no place at all for the New Testament or any part of it. They consider it, the writing, I mean the books themselves, each individual book was practically in every case written by a Jew or a former Jew, but it is not part of the Jewish tradition and sometimes certain portions of it are distinctly offensive to Jewish tradition.

* * *

Q. Dr. Grayzel, I will ask you. You said at the end of your last answer that it would be regarded as offensive. How would you describe it, the word "offensive" having connotations both of a religious and non-religious nature, how would you describe it, what would be the words that you describe it from the religious standpoint? What would it be called, the concept of the divinity of Christ?

A. I don't want to step on anybody's toes, but the idea of God having a son is, from the viewpoint of Jewish faith, practically blasphemous.

Q. And was that concept, in the view of the Jewish faith, the assertion by Christ of divinity in that sense of the word, the crime of Christ in the view of the Jewish church at the time?

A. If that incident happened, I mean Jesus—

Q. If the incident happened would it have been such assertion?

A. It would have been offensive, yes.

   By Judge Biggs:

Q. Would it have been blasphemous?

A. Blasphemous, yes.

* * *

Q. Could I invite your attention, Doctor, and ask you to comment on any differences that you find in Isaiah 7:14?

A. Yes. The 7th Chapter of Isaiah speaks of a situation in which the prophet pointed to or expressed himself, "Behold, a virgin shall conceive, and bear a son, and call his name Immanuel."

Q. Now, what version are you reading from there, sir?

A. This is the King James version.

Q. How does that language appear in the Jewish—

A. In the, in our version, it reads, "Behold, the young woman shall conceive and bear a son and shall call his name Immanuel." It is "the" and "young woman."

Now, the translation "young woman" was in this instance accepted by the revised standard version. Not all Christian sects have approved, but in this instance the old Jewish translation was accepted, but they still say, "a young woman," which is admissible from the point of view of the Hebrew text. But there we come up against a distinct difference in religious faith. The Jewish attitude was that the prophet was speaking about a situation which existed right in front of him. The king had a young wife and she was pregnant and the prophet turned to the king and said, "Now, this young woman who has conceived," or if she wasn't pregnant, "will conceive and she will bear a child and his name should be," as we interpret it poetically speaking "Immanuel," which is the Hebrew for "God is with us."

Now, the Christian church subsequently took this, as it did any number of other passages, as a prophecy, a prediction of things that were to happen many centuries later, and took the words "young woman," which could be from the Hebrew viewpoint, could be either a married young woman or an unmarried young woman, took it to be a virgin. And so you have here an example, one of the basic examples of deviations between the two, the differences between the two faiths.

Q. Now, Doctor, as a rabbi, could you comment on the religious aspects from the standpoint of Jewish faith of necessarily reading the Bible without comment?

A. Again, here is a difference in attitude. I don't know to what extent it is prevalent among Christians at the present time. In Judaism the Bible is not read, it is studied. There is no special virtue attached to a mere reading of the Bible; there is a great deal of virtue attached to a study of the Bible. And it, therefore, always strikes me, speaking for myself, as rather peculiar that anything such as reading the Bible should be an important matter. I can understand, and let me, to make my position clear, I want to state it quite firmly, that I think it is most important for Christian children or Christian adults to read and to study the Bible, to study it. But as soon as you begin studying the Bible in the school, of course, there you have a distinct violation of a basic principle of Americansim.

* * *

Q. Let me put my question this way: As a rabbi, are you familiar with instances in which confusion has arisen in the minds of children with whom you have come in contact as a rabbi as a result of the mere reading of the Bible without explanatory comment or interpretation by somebody authorized and qualified to do so in the Jewish faith, and if so could you give us such an example?

A. If I may answer that question, I would like to cite, with all due respect to Mr. Schempp who testified just a little while ago, the statement that he made, and indicate how the Bible is misunderstood when it is taken without explanation. I mean this reference to a passage in the Bible in Leviticus, which certainly is rarely read, but if an animal is found dead, killed or died naturally, that a Jew may not eat it but a non-Jew may.

Now, if you study the passage it becomes perfectly clear that it was not an act of contempt for the non-Jew but an act of further sanctification for the Jew. He was to abide by certain rules. But since the non-Jew in those days, and presumably now, wouldn't hesitate to eat that kind of animal, you are not to deprive him of it. But as a Jew you are not supposed to eat it. Now, that does not come out from a mere reading of the Bible, but it does come out from a study of the Bible, and there are any number of such instances.

Judge Kirkpatrick: You were asked about the particular cases of children that you were familiar with who were confused.

The Witness: Yes. Now, there are children who have come to me, I mean Jewish children, naturally, who have come to me and on some occasions—I used to be a teacher, too. That I didn't say before—and told me that or asked for explanations of certain readings which were made to them and which led to discussions afterwards with their fellow students, much to their dismay because their answers just came out second best.

For example, such a simple story as the sale of the birthright by Esau to Jacob. Now, if you read the passage as it is written, without paying too much attention to it, it is possible, as happened, for a child, for a non-Jewish child to come to a Jewish friend and say, "I see now your ancestor was a cheat. He took advantage of his brother who came in tired and hungry and made him give up something valuable for a mess of pottage."

But the point of the story, which I had to—I remember having to explain to the complaining child—was the last phrase in it. The point was, "Thus, Esau despised his birthright."

It wasn't the question of whether Jacob took advantage of him or not; the point of the story is that Esau had so little regard for his birthright that he was ready to sell it or give it away for a petty thing.

* * *

Q. Now, to move on again, Doctor, by specifically calling your attention to a passage, would you refer in the King James version to portions of Matthew 23, which, to refresh all of our recollections, I would ask you first to read and then to comment upon from the standpoint of the Jewish faith and, secondly, from the standpoint of the reaction of a Jewish child, if it's been within your experience, to that passage.

A. Well, in Matthew 23 we have an address of Jesus about his contemporary Jews, and in several portions of that chapter he says—I am reading Verse 13 from the King James version—"But woe unto you Scribes and Pharisees, hypocrites! For ye shut up the Kingdom of Heaven against men," and so on, and then that's repeated later on in the various, where he makes various points. And it seems perfectly clear that a Jewish child subjected to this kind of reading, and finding that his, the traditional leaders of his religion, are being called hypocrites by the most important personality of the religion of the other children, are not going to be very happy about it.

Q. And how about Matthew 26, sir?

A. Is it 26? No. It is—I think you refer to Chapter 27.

Q. I am sorry.

A. Which discusses—

Q. The scene of the conviction.

A. —the crucifixion and the conviction. And the scene is, if you recall, where he appears, where Pilate, Pontius Pilate comes out on the balcony of his palace and asks the crowd down below whether they would choose that he release Jesus—may I read—which is called Christ and, or Barabbas, who was a thief. And Verse 22: "Pilate saith unto them, What shall I do then with Jesus which is called Christ? They all say unto him, Let him be crucified.

"And the governor said, Why, what evil hath he done? But they cried out the more, saying, Let him be crucified."

And then when Pilate saw that he couldn't prevail, he washed his hands and said that he is clear of this sin.

"Then answered all the people, and said, His blood be on us, and on our children."

And I submit to you that this verse, this exclamation has been the cause of more anti-Jewish riots throughout the ages than anything else in history. And if you subject a Jewish child to listening to this sort of reading, which is not at all unlikely before Christmas or before Easter —rather, before Easter, I think he is being subjected to little short of torture.

* * *

Q. Did you also have occasion to have it come to your attention as to the effect upon these children of religious matter having to do with the story of Christ and his crucifixion?

A. Oh, well, there is a very interesting psychological situation in the case of Jewish children. They are brought up in the midst of a Christian environment. The story of Christianity obviously plays some part in their contacts both in the outside world with their friends and certainly within the school, within the environs of the school. It is inevitable and certainly part of their education—I don't think it is possible to expect anything else—that something of the story of the origin of Christianity should be taught or should be discussed.

Very much depends—I am talking now from the viewpoint of the Jewish child and its attitudes and its adjustment to the outside world; its happiness, in whatever term you want to apply to it, is very important how this story is told, how it is taught, and how the child's friends react to it. Given an intelligent teacher—Jewish, Protestant, Catholic, it doesn't matter—given an intelligent teacher that story can be taught in such a way as to leave no scars on the consciousness of the child. I don't know how many such teachers there are.

The story itself lends itself to being told in such fashion as to act as a divisive force within the children's—within the society, within the social milieu of the school. And I have had any number of instances where a pupil of mine, let us say here at Gratz College, a high school pupil, would come very much disturbed at the way the story was presented to him.

I am not talking about Bible reading, I mean the way the story is presented, whether in connection with the Bible or not, I don't know. And this passage, for example, to which I referred yesterday, from Matthew 27, is one of the crucial passages.

Q. Now, Doctor, if the passage alone were read in the absence of the kind of instruction and the kind of explanation which you say is possible, what then in your experience would be the reaction of the Jewish child?

A. I think that without explanation this is a very, very serious matter. I think it can be explained. I think it should be explained. If a teacher reads it in class or wants to tell the story with this passage as part of it, you cannot, I mean, erase it from the Bible, from the New Testament. But given an explanation it can be put in its place and can leave less harmful effect. But without explanation, I think it is a direct accusation and a threat which is very disturbing.

The case for the defendant school district relied, first, on several officials of the Pennsylvania school system, who testified as to the various procedures and regulations for Bible-reading in the Pennsylvania public schools. The school district then called one other witness— Dr. Luther Weigle, the former Dean of the Yale Divinity School, and Chairman of the Committee which recently prepared the new Revised Standard Version of the Bible.

On direct examination, Dean Weigle testified, in part, as follows:

Q. Dean Weigle, coming to the issues in this case, there is a statute in Pennsylvania which provides—and I am merely summarizing it—that there shall be read in the public schools of this Commonwealth ten verses of the Holy Bible without comment at the opening of school.

May I ask you whether you have any opinion as to whether the reading of ten verses of the King James Version of the Bible without comment is sectarian in character?

A. In my opinion, because the Bible is not a sectarian book, that practice is not sectarian.

Q. Would that answer be the same, Dean Weigle, if there were a reading in the same manner as I have described from the Douay Version of the Bible?

A. The same.

Q. Would the same apply if the reading were from the Jewish Version of the Bible which you have identified a moment ago?

A. The same.

* * *

By Judge Kirkpatrick:

Q. May I ask a question. Do you think that if a teacher by chance happened to be a person of the Jewish faith and he eliminated the King James Version entirely from the school, didn't permit anybody to read anything from the King James Version and only allowed readings from the Scriptures, the Hebrew Scriptures, in English, of course, do you think that he would be conducting exercises which involved the reading of verses from the Holy Bible?

A. He would certainly be conducting exercises which would involve the reading of the Holy Scriptures, as he understands the Holy Scriptures.

Q. But the trouble is the law says the Holy Bible is what must be read.

A. Yes. His practice would be sectarian practice.

By Mr. Rhoads:

Q. If he permitted nothing else, you mean?

A. Yes, if he permitted nothing else.

Judge Kirkpatrick: Yes, that is what I inquired.

Q. Now, Dean Weigle, based upon your experience as an educator, have you formed any opinion as to whether, from the educational standpoint, the reading of ten verses of the Holy Bible as described in this case—and by "The Holy Bible" for the minute I will refer to the King James Standard Version—do you believe that that possesses any educational value?

A. I do.

Q. What kind of educational value do you think it possesses, sir?

A. It possesses a moral educational value because, after all, the Bible is the record of the experience of the people that discovered what God really is like, and has given us the Ten commandments and other moral precepts which are contained in the Holy Bible.

It is of very high literary value because the King James Bible is what one authority has called the noblest monument of English prose. It has contributed to the making of the English language as no other English book has done.

It is of great value, it seems to me, to the perpetuation of those institutions and those practices which we ideally think of as the American way of life, because the Bible has entered vitally into the stream of American life.

I won't stop to say anything more than that Lincoln was an assiduous student of the Bible; that much that Lincoln did and much that Lincoln wrote bears the stamp of his understanding of the Bible upon it.

We have recently had a book by a man who has investigated the early fathers, in which he finds that among all of them, Franklin, Washington, Jefferson, Madison, John Adams, though they were men that were far from the strictest orthodoxy or far from being adherents to everything for which institutional religion stands, they had this supreme reverence for the Bible.

Those are my reasons, sir.

* * *

Q. Dean Weigle, there is one phase of the case which I have neglected to advert to in my questioning. There is also the practice in Abington School District of reciting the Lord's Prayer at the same opening exercises. Have you any observations as to that practice, sir?

A. It seems to me to be an entirely seemly and proper practice. After all, it is very much like the opening of legislative assemblies with prayer.

I see nothing in the Lord's Prayer that is sectarian. Everything in that prayer can be paralleled in Jewish literature, in the Holy Scriptures of the Jewish people.

On cross-examination by the Schempp's attorney, Dean Weigle testified, in part, as follows:

Q. Dean, the New Revised Standard Version of which you spoke in the early part of your testimony was greeted with some controversy in the Protestant world, is that correct?

A. No, it wasn't greeted with any controversy in the Protestant world. It received some controversy from certain fringes, but—

Q. What were those fringes?

A. —it has been—

Mr. Rhoades: Just wait. Let him answer, please.

A. It has been welcomed very heartily in the Protestant world.

By Mr. Sawyer:

Q. What were the fringes that you speak of that took exception to the New Revised Version?

A. Well, people who thought that there ought to be no revision.

* * *

Q. Now, did there come a time, sir, if you know, when there was a burning of the Revised Standard Version a few weeks after it was published in December of 1952, down in North Carolina? Do you remember that incident?

A. Yes.

Q. Do you recall that one of the things that was attacked was the fact that in, I believe it is Isaiah 7:14, the New Revised Standard substitutes the word "woman" for the word "virgin" in speaking of the prophecy of Isaiah which the Christian Church has widely acclaimed and heralded in the coming of Christ? Is that an incident which is familiar to you, sir?

A. Yes.

* * *

Q. Would you say, sir, that in the translation of Isaiah 7:14, that there is no sectarian aspect as to whether or not one believes that the word of God there set forth is that a young virgin shall conceive or a young woman shall conceive? Is that a sectarian issue?

A. That is not a sectarian issue.

May I ask a bit of liberty to speak to that, sir?

Judge Biggs: Yes, you may.

A. (Continuing) The doctrine of the virgin birth so far as the Scriptures, so far as the Holy Bible is concerned, rests upon various direct statements which are made in the New Testament, in Matthew and in Luke. It does not depend upon the translation of that particular text in Isaiah.

The Bible itself, of course, at that point is the Hebrew. A translation is just a translation. It chanced that the Septuagint used there as translation for the Hebrew word "almah," which means young woman—

By Judge Kirkpatrick:

Q. How do you spell that, please?

A. A-l-m-a-h. The Hebrew has a-l-m-a-h, which means young woman. It chanced that the Septuagint used at that place the Greek word "parthenos." The usual meaning of parthenos is virgin, but the Greek Septuagint is very loose in its use of the word "parthenos." For example, it calls Dinah a parthenos after Schechem had raped her.

The translation of this word by scholars generally is young woman. It has been so accepted by all of the basic Hebrew dictionaries. It has been accepted by Fundamentalist scholars who may have objected to other points of the Revised Standard Version but do not object to this. It has been accepted by churches that, well, you wouldn't expect to accept it.

By Mr. Sawyer:

Q. Has it been rejected by others?

A. I don't know anyone that has rejected it that understands the Hebrew.

Q. I am not asking you whether they are wrong or right in their reactions, as your answer was, sir, but do you know that there are bodies of opinion within the Protestant world and outside of it which specifically rejected this translation?

A. Oh, yes.

Q. Doctor, would you say that the Holy Bible—and I am using those particular words—the Holy Bible would be complete without the New Testament?

A. No.

Q. You defined, I believe, a sectarian Bible as one in which the message of a particular sect were conveyed by that version of the Bible. On that definition, Doctor, would you say that the New Testament was sectarian in that it conveys the message of a particular sect?

A. It conveys the message of Christians.

Q. Yes, as opposed to non-Christian sects?

A. Yes.

Q. When you said "non-sectarian," did you mean as among the various Protestant sects?

A. I meant among the various Christian bodies.

* * *

Q. On page 127 of your book, you recount an incident in which someone invited your attention to—well, I will read it to you, sir.

A. Sure.

Q. "Much of what is said as to the value of the King James Version for use in worship is without any sound basis. One man argued that we should always say, 'Our Father which art in heaven' because the word 'which' removes God from the company of men, and sets him apart as unique and transcendent. The King James translators would have laughed at such an interpretation; for them the relative pronoun 'which' has the meaning that the relative pronoun 'who' now has."

So isn't that an example, Doctor, of where a word may make a difference as to whether or not you are a Transcendentalist or whether or not the God which you imagine is anthropomorphic?

A. Oh, no; oh, no. After all, when the King James Version people said "Our Father which art in heaven" they meant exactly the same thing that we mean by "Our Father who art in heaven." There certainly is no controversy on that point.

This particular man to whom I referred is an eccentric in his feeling that "which" makes God transcendent.

Q. He is at least one, is he not, Doctor?

A. Yes. I had that controversy with him.

Q. It did make a difference to him, didn't it?

A. Perhaps.

Both the Schempp and Murray cases were argued together before the Supreme Court in February of 1963, and on June 17, the Court rendered one decision to resolve both cases.

We now reproduce in full the entire text of the majority, concurring and dissenting opinions, exactly as they appear in the slip sheet reports of the United States Supreme Court.

SUPREME COURT OF THE UNITED STATES

Nos. 142 AND 119.—OCTOBER TERM, 1962.

School District of Abington Township, Pennsylvania, et al., Appellants, 142 *v.* Edward Lewis Schempp et al.	On Appeal From the United States District Court for the Eastern District of Pennsylvania.
William J. Murray III, etc., et al., Petitioners, 119; *v.* John N. Curlett, President, et al., Individually, and Constituting the Board of School Commissioners of Baltimore City.	On Writ of Certiorari to the Court of Appeals of Maryland.

[June 17, 1963.]

MR. JUSTICE CLARK delivered the opinion of the Court.

Once again we are called upon to consider the scope of the provision of the First Amendment to the United States Constitution which declares that "Congress shall make no law respecting an establishment of religion or prohibiting the free exercise thereof . . . ." These companion cases present the issues in the context of state action requiring that schools begin each day with readings from the Bible. While raising the basic questions under slightly different factual situations, the cases permit of joint treatment. In light of the history of the First Amendment and of our cases interpreting and applying its requirements, we hold that the practices at issue and the laws requiring them are unconstitutional under the Establishment Clause, as applied to the states through the Fourteenth Amendment.

I.

The Facts in Each Case: No. 142. The Commonwealth of Pennsylvania by law, 24 Pa. Stat. § 15–1516, as amended, Pub. Law 1928 (Supp. 1960) Dec. 17, 1959, requires that "At least ten verses from the Holy Bible shall be read, without comment, at the opening of each public school on each school day. Any child shall be excused from such Bible reading, or attending such Bible reading, upon the written request of his parent or guardian." The Schempp family, husband and wife and two of their three children, brought suit to enjoin enforcement of the statute, contending that their rights under the Fourteenth Amendment to the Constitution of the United States are, have been, and will continue to be violated unless this statute be declared unconstitutional as violative of these provisions of the First Amendment. They sought to enjoin the appellant school district, wherein the Schempp children attend school, and its officers and the Superintendent of Public Instruction of the Commonwealth from continuing to conduct such readings and recitation of the Lord's Prayer in the public schools of the district pursuant to the statute. A three-judge statutory District Court for the Eastern District of Pennsylvania held that the statute is violative of the Establishment Clause of the First Amendment as applied to the States by the Due Process Clause of the Fourteenth Amendment and directed that appropriate injunctive relief issue. 201 F. Supp. 815.[1] On appeal by the District, its officials and

---

[1] The action was brought in 1958, prior to the 1959 amendment of § 15–1516 authorizing a child's nonattendance at the exercises upon parental request. The three-judge court held the statute and the practices complained of unconstitutional under both the Establishment Clause and the Free Exercise Clause. 177 F. Supp. 398. Pending appeal to this Court by the school district, the statute was so amended, and we vacated the judgment and remanded for further

the Superintendent, under 28 U. S. C. § 1253, we noted probable jurisdiction. 371 U. S. 807.

The appellees Edward Lewis Schempp, his wife Sidney, and their children, Roger and Donna, are of the Unitarian faith and are members of the Unitarian Church in Germantown, Philadelphia, Pennsylvania, where they, as well as another son, Ellory, regularly attend religious services. The latter was originally a party but having graduated from the school.system *pendente lite* was voluntarily dismissed from the action. The other children attend the Abington Senior High School, which is a public school operated by appellant district.

On each school day at the Abington Senior High School between 8:15 and 8:30 a. m., while the pupils are attending their home rooms or advisory sections, opening exercises are conducted pursuant to the statute. The exercises are broadcast into each room in the school building through an intercommunications system and are conducted under the supervision of a teacher by students attending the school's radio and television workshop. Selected students from this course gather each morning in the school's workshop studio for the exercises, which include readings by one of the students of 10 verses of the Holy Bible, broadcast to each room in the building. This is followed by the recitation of the Lord's Prayer, likewise over the intercommunications system, but also by the students in the various classrooms, who are asked to stand and join in repeating the prayer in unison. The exercises are closed with the flag salute and such pertinent announcements as are of interest to the students. Participation in the opening exercises, as directed by the statute, is voluntary. The student reading the verses

---

proceedings. 364 U. S. 298. The same three-judge court granted appellees' motion to amend the pleadings, 195 F. Supp. 518, held a hearing on the amended pleadings and rendered the judgment, 201 F. Supp. 815, from which appeal is now taken.

from the Bible may select the passages and read from any version he chooses, although the only copies furnished by the school are the King James version, copies of which were circulated to each teacher by the school district. During the period in which the exercises have been conducted the King James, the Douay and the Revised Standard versions of the Bible have been used, as well as the Jewish Holy Scriptures. There are no prefatory statements, no questions asked or solicited, no comments or explanations made and no interpretations given at or during the exercises. The students and parents are advised that the student may absent himself from the classroom or, should he elect to remain, not participate in the exercises.

It appears from the record that in schools not having an intercommunications system the Bible reading and the recitation of the Lord's Prayer were conducted by the home-room teacher,[2] who chose the text of the verses and read them herself or had students read them in rotation or by volunteers. This was followed by a standing recitation of the Lord's Prayer, together with the Pledge of Allegiance to the flag by the class in unison and a closing announcement of routine school items of interest.

At the first trial Edward Schempp and the children testified as to specific religious doctrines purveyed by a literal reading of the Bible "which were contrary to the religious beliefs which they held and to their familial teaching." 177 F. Supp. 398, 400. The children testified that all of the doctrines to which they referred were read to them at various times as part of the exercises. Edward Schempp testified at the second trial that he had considered having Roger and Donna excused from at-

---

[2] The statute as amended imposes no penalty upon a teacher refusing to obey its mandate. However, it remains to be seen whether one refusing could have his contract of employment terminated for "wilful violation of the school laws." 24 Pa. Stat. (Supp. 1960) § 11–1122.

tendance at the exercises but decided against it for several reasons, including his belief that the children's relationships with their teachers and classmates would be adversely affected.[3]

Expert testimony was introduced by both appellants and appellees at the first trial, which testimony was summarized by the trial court as follows:

"Dr. Solomon Grayzel testified that there were marked differences between the Jewish Holy Scriptures and the Christian Holy Bible, the most obvious of which was the absence of the New Testament in the Jewish Holy Scriptures. Dr. Grayzel testified that portions of the New Testament were offensive to Jewish tradition and that, from the standpoint of Jewish faith, the concept of Jesus Christ as the Son of God was 'practically blasphemous.' He cited instances in the New Testament which, assertedly, were not only sectarian in nature but tended to bring the Jews into ridicule or scorn. Dr. Grayzel gave

---

[3] The trial court summarized his testimony as follows:

"Edward Schempp, the children's father, testified that after careful consideration he had decided that he should not have Roger or Donna excused from attendance at these morning ceremonies. Among his reasons were the following. He said that he thought his children would be 'labeled as "odd balls"' before their teachers and classmates every school day; that children, like Roger's and Donna's classmates, were liable 'to lump all particular religious difference[s] or religious objections [together] as "atheism"' and that today the word 'atheism' is often connected with 'atheistic communism,' and has 'very bad' connotations, such as 'un-American' or 'anti-Red,' with overtones of possible immorality. Mr. Schempp pointed out that due to the events of the morning exercises following in rapid succession, the Bible reading, the Lord's Prayer, the Flag Salute, and the announcements, excusing his children from the Bible reading would mean that probably they would miss hearing the announcements so important to children. He testified also that if Roger and Donna were excused from Bible reading they would have to stand in the hall outside their 'homeroom' and that this carried with it the imputation of punishment for bad conduct." 201 F. Supp., at 818.

as his expert opinion that such material from the New Testament could be explained to Jewish children in such a way as to do no harm to them. But if pörtions of the New Testament were read without explanation, they could be, and in his specific experience with children Dr. Grayzel observed, had been, psychologically harmful to the child and had caused a divisive force within the social media of the school.

"Dr. Grayzel also testified that there was significant difference in attitude with regard to the respective Books of the Jewish and Christian Religions in that Judaism attaches no special significance to the reading of the Bible *per se* and that the Jewish Holy Scriptures are source materials to be studied. But Dr. Grayzel did state that many portions of the New, as well as of the Old, Testament contained passages of great literary and moral value.

"Dr. Luther A. Weigle, an expert witness for the defense, testified in some detail as to the reasons for and the methods employed in developing the King James and the Revised Standard Versions of the Bible. On direct examination, Dr. Weigle stated that the Bible was non-sectarian. He later stated that the phrase 'non-sectarian' meant to him non-sectarian within the Christian faiths. Dr. Weigle stated that his definition of the Holy Bible would include the Jewish Holy Scriptures, but also stated that the 'Holy Bible' would not be complete without the New Testament. He stated that the New Testament 'conveyed the message of Christians.' In his opinion, reading of the Holy Scriptures to the exclusion of the New Testament would be a sectarian practice. Dr. Weigle stated that the Bible was of great moral, historical and literary value. This is conceded by all the parties and is also the view of the court." 177 F. Supp. 398, 401–402.

The trial court, in striking down the practices and the statute requiring them, made specific findings of fact that the children's attendance at Abington Senior High School is compulsory and that the practice of reading 10 verses from the Bible is also compelled by law. It also found that:

> "The reading of the verses, even without comment, possesses a devotional and religious character and constitutes in effect a religious observance. The devotional and religious nature of the morning exercises is made all the more apparent by the fact that the Bible reading is followed immediately by a recital in unison by the pupils of the Lord's Prayer. The fact that some pupils, or theoretically all pupils, might be excused from attendance at the exercises does not mitigate the obligatory nature of the ceremony for . . . Section 1516 . . . unequivocally requires the exercises to be held every school day in every school in the Commonwealth. The exercises are held in the school buildings and perforce are conducted by and under the authority of the local school authorities and during school sessions. Since the statute requires the reading of the 'Holy Bible,' a Christian document, the practice . . . prefers the Christian religion. The record demonstrates that it was the intention of . . . the Commonwealth . . . to introduce a religious ceremony into the public schools of the Commonwealth." 201 F. Supp., at 819.

No. 119. In 1905 the Board of School Commissioners of Baltimore City adopted a rule pursuant to Art. 77, § 202 of the Annotated Code of Maryland. The rule provided for the holding of opening exercises in the schools of the city consisting primarily of the "reading, without comment, of a chapter in the Holy Bible and/or the use of the Lord's Prayer." The petitioners, Mrs. Madalyn Murray and her son, William J. Murray, III, are both professed atheists. Following unsuccessful attempts to have the respondent school board rescind the rule this suit was filed for mandamus to compel its rescission and cancellation. It was alleged that William was a student in a public school of the city and Mrs. Murray, his mother, was a taxpayer therein; that it was the practice under the rule to have a reading on each school morning from the King James version of the Bible; that at petitioners' insistence the rule was amended [4] to permit children to be excused from the exercise on request of the parent and that William had been excused pursuant thereto; that nevertheless the rule as amended was in violation of the petitioners' rights "to freedom of religion under the First and Fourteenth Amendments" and in violation of "the principle of separation between church and state, contained therein. . . ." The petition particularized the petitioners' atheistic beliefs and stated that the rule, as practiced, violated their rights

> "in that it threatens their religious liberty by placing a premium on belief as against non-belief and subjects their freedom of conscience to the rule of the majority; it pronounces belief in God as the source of all moral and spiritual values, equating these values with religious values, and thereby renders sinister,

---

[4] The rule as amended provides as follows:

"Opening Exercise. Each school, either collectively or in classes, shall be opened by the reading, without comment, of a chapter in the Holy Bible and/or the use of the Lord's Prayer. The Douay version may be used by those pupils who prefer it. Appropriate patriotic exercises should be held as a part of the general opening exercise of the school or class. Any child shall be excused from participating in the opening exercises or from attending the opening exercises upon written request of his parent or guardian."

alien and suspect the beliefs and ideals of . . . . Petitioners, promoting doubt and question of their morality, good citizenship and good faith."

The respondents demurred and the trial court, recognizing that the demurrer admitted all facts well pleaded, sustained it without leave to amend. The Maryland Court of Appeals affirmed, the majority of four justices holding the exercise not in violation of the First and Fourteenth Amendments, with three justices dissenting. 228 Md. 239, 179 A. 2d 698. We granted certiorari. 371 U. S. 809.

II.

It is true that religion has been closely identified with our history and government. As we said in *Engel* v. *Vitale,* 370 U. S. 421, 434 (1962), "The history of man is inseparable from the history of religion. And . . . since the beginning of that history many people have devoutly believed that 'More things are wrought by prayer than this world dreams of.' " In *Zorach* v. *Clauson,* 343 U. S. 306, 313 (1952), we gave specific recognition to the proposition that "[w]e are a religious people whose institutions presuppose a Supreme Being." The fact that the Founding Fathers believed devotedly that there was a God and that the unalienable rights of man were rooted in Him is clearly evidenced in their writings, from the Mayflower Compact to the Constitution itself. This background is evidenced today in our public life through the continuance in our oaths of office from the Presidency to the Alderman of the final supplication, "So help me God." Likewise each House of the Congress provides through its Chaplain an opening prayer, and the sessions of this Court are declared open by the crier in a short ceremony, the final phrase of which invokes the grace of God. Again, there are such manifestations in our military forces, where those of our citizens who are under the restrictions of military service wish to engage in voluntary worship. Indeed, only last year an official survey of the country indicated that 64% of our people have church membership, Bureau of Census, U. S. Department of Commerce, Statistical Abstract of the United States, 48 (83d ed. 1962), while less than 3% profess no religion whatever. *Id.,* at p. 46. It can be truly said, therefore, that today, as in the beginning, our national life reflects a religious people who, in the words of Madison, are "earnestly praying, as . . . in duty bound, that the Supreme Lawgiver of the Universe . . . guide them into every measure which may be worthy of his . . . blessing . . . ." Memorial and Remonstrance Against Religious Assessments, quoted in *Everson* v. *Board of Education,* 330 U. S. 1, 71–72 (1947) (Appendix to dissenting opinion of Rutledge, J.).

This is not to say, however, that religion has been so identified with our history and government that religious freedom is not likewise as strongly imbedded in our public and private life. Nothing but the most telling of personal experiences in religious persecution suffered by our forebears, see *Everson* v. *Board of Education, supra,* at 8–11, could have planted our belief in liberty of religious opinion any more deeply in our heritage. It is true that this liberty frequently was not realized by the colonists, but this is readily accountable to their close ties to the Mother Country.[5] However, the views of Madison and Jefferson, preceded by Roger Williams,[6] came to be incor-

---

[5] There were established churches in at least eight of the original colonies, and various degrees of religious support in others as late as the Revolutionary War. See *Engel* v. *Vitale, supra,* at 428, n. 10.

[6] "There goes many a ship to sea, with many hundred souls in one ship, whose weal and woe is common, and is a true picture of a commonwealth, or human combination, or society. It hath fallen out sometimes, that both Papists and Protestants, Jews and Turks, may be embarked in one ship; upon which supposal, I affirm that all the liberty of conscience I ever pleaded for, turns upon these two

porated not only in the Federal Constitution but likewise in those of most of our States.   This freedom to worship was indispensable in a country whose people came from the four quarters of the earth and brought with them a diversity of religious opinion. . Today authorities list 83 separate religious bodies, each with memberships exceeding 50,000, existing among our people, as well as innumerable smaller groups.   Bureau of Census, *op. cit., supra,* at 46–47.

III.

Almost a hundred years ago in *Minor* v. *Board of Education of Cincinnati,*[7] Judge Alphonzo Taft, father of the revered Chief Justice, in an unpublished opinion stated the ideal of our people as to religious freedom as one of

> "absolute equality before the law of all religious opinions and sects . . . ."

.   .   .   .   .

> "The government is neutral, and, while protecting all, it prefers none, and it disparages none."

Before examining this "neutral" position in which the Establishment and Free Exercise Clauses of the First Amendment place our government it is well that we discuss the reach of the Amendment under the cases of this Court.

---

hinges, that none of the Papists, Protestants, Jews, or Turks be forced to come to the ship's prayers or worship, nor compelled from their own particular prayers or worship, if they practice any."

[7] Superior Court of Cincinnati, February 1870.   The opinion is not reported but is published under the title, The Bible in the Common Schools (Cincinnati: Robert Clarke & Co. 1870).   Judge Taft's views, expressed in dissent, prevailed on appeal.   See *Board of Education of Cincinnati* v. *Minor*, 23 Ohio St. 211, 253 (1872), in which the Ohio Supreme Court held that:

"The great bulk of human affairs and human interests is left by any free government to individual enterprise and individual action.   Religion is eminently one of these interests, lying outside the true and legitimate province of government."

First, this Court has decisively settled that the First Amendment's mandate that "Congress shall make no law respecting an establishment of religion, or prohibiting the free exercise thereof" has been made wholly applicable to the states by the Fourteenth Amendment. Twenty-three years ago in *Cantwell* v. *Connecticut,* 310 U. S. 296, 303 (1940), this Court, through Mr. Justice Roberts, said:

> "The fundamental concept of liberty embodied in that [Fourteenth] Amendment embraces the liberties guaranteed by the First Amendment. The First Amendment declares that Congress shall make no law respecting an establishment of religion or prohibiting the free exercise thereof. The Fourteenth Amendment has rendered the legislatures of the states as incompetent as Congress to enact such laws . . . ." [8]

In a series of cases since *Cantwell* the Court has repeatedly reaffirmed that doctrine, and we do so now. *Murdock* v. *Pennsylvania,* 319 U. S. 105, 108 (1943); *Everson* v. *Board of Education, supra; Illinois ex rel. McCollum* v. *Board of Education,* 333 U. S. 203, 210–211 (1948); *Zorach* v. *Clauson, supra; McGowan* v. *Maryland,* 366 U. S. 420 (1961); *Torcaso* v. *Watkins,* 367 U. S. 488 (1961); and *Engel* v. *Vitale, supra.*

Second, this Court has rejected unequivocally the contention that the establishment clause forbids only governmental preference of one religion over another. Al-

---

[8] Application to the States of other clauses of the First Amendment obtained even before *Cantwell.* Almost 40 years ago in the opinion of the Court in *Gitlow* v. *New York,* 268 U. S. 652, 666 (1925), Mr. Justice Sanford said: "For present purposes we may and do assume that freedom of speech and of the press—which are protected by the First Amendment from abridgement by Congress—are among the fundamental personal rights and 'liberties' protected by the Due Process Clause of the Fourteenth Amendment from impairment by the States."

most 20 years ago in *Everson, supra,* at 15, the Court said that "[n]either a state nor the Federal government can set up a church. Neither can pass laws which aid one religion, aid all religions, or prefer one religion over another." And Mr. Justice Jackson, dissenting, agreed:

"There is no answer to the proposition . . . that the effect of the religious freedom Amendment to our Constitution was to take every form of propagation of religion out of the realm of things which could directly or indirectly be made public business and thereby be supported in whole or in part at taxpayers' expense . . . . This freedom was first in the Bill of Rights because it was first in the forefathers' minds; it was set forth in absolute terms, and its strength is its rigidity." *Id.,* at 26.

Further, Mr. Justice Rutledge, joined by Justices Frankfurter, Jackson and Burton, declared:

"The [First] Amendment's purpose was not to strike merely at the official establishment of a single sect, creed or religion, outlawing only a formal relation such as had prevailed in England and some of the Colonies. Necessarily it was to uproot all such relationships. But the object was broader than separating church and state in this narrow sense. It was to create a complete and permanent separation of the spheres of religious activity and civil authority by comprehensively forbidding every form of public aid or support for religion." *Id.,* at 31–32.

The same conclusion has been firmly maintained ever since that time, see *Illinois ex rel. McCollum, supra,* at pp. 210–211; *McGowan* v. *Maryland, supra,* at 442–443; *Torcaso* v. *Watkins, supra,* at 492–493, 495, and we reaffirm it now.

While none of the parties to either of these cases has questioned these basic conclusions of the Court, both of which have been long established, recognized and consistently reaffirmed, others continue to question their history, logic and efficacy. Such contentions, in the light of the consistent interpretation in cases of this Court, seem entirely untenable and of value only as academic exercises.

IV.

The interrelationship of the Establishment and the Free Exercise Clauses was first touched upon by Mr. Justice Roberts for the Court in *Cantwell* v. *Connecticut, supra,* at 303, where it was said that their "inhibition of legislation" had

> "a double aspect. On the one hand, it forestalls compulsion by law of the acceptance of any creed or the practice of any form of worship. Freedom of conscience and freedom to adhere to such religious organization or form of worship as the individual may choose cannot be restricted by law. On the other hand, it safeguards the free exercise of the chosen form of religion. Thus the Amendment embraces two concepts—freedom to believe and freedom to act. The first is absolute but, in the nature of things, the second cannot be."

A half dozen years later in *Everson* v. *Board of Education, supra,* at 14–15, this Court, through MR. JUSTICE BLACK, stated that the "scope of the First Amendment . . . was designed forever to suppress" the establishment of religion or the prohibition of the free exercise thereof. In short, the Court held that the Amendment

> "requires the state to be a neutral in its relations with groups of religious believers and non-believers; it does not require the state to be their adversary. State power is no more to be used so as to handicap religions than it is to favor them." *Id.,* at 18.

And Mr. Justice Jackson, in dissent, declared that public schools are organized

> "on the premise that secular education can be iso-
> lated from all religious teaching so that the school
> can inculcate all needed temporal knowledge and also
> maintain a strict and lofty neutrality as to religion.
> The assumption is that after the individual has been
> instructed in worldly wisdom he will be better fitted
> to choose his religion." *Id.,* at 23–24.

Moreover, all of the four dissenters, speaking through Mr. Justice Rutledge, agreed that

> "Our constitutional policy . . . . [D]oes not deny
> the value or necessity for religious training, teaching
> or observance.   Rather it secures their free exercise.
> But to that end it does deny that the state can under-
> take or sustain them in any form or degree.   For this
> reason the sphere of religious activity, as distin-
> guished from the secular intellectual liberties, has
> been given the two-fold protection and, as the state
> cannot forbid, neither can it perform or aid in per-
> forming the religious function.   The dual prohibition
> makes that function altogether private." *Id.,* at 52.

Only one year later the Court was asked to reconsider and repudiate the doctrine of these cases in *McCollum* v. *Board of Education.* It was argued that "historically the First Amendment was intended to forbid only govern-ment preference of one religion over another . . . . In addition they ask that we distinguish or overrule our hold-ing in the *Everson* case that the Fourteenth Amendment made the 'establishment of religion' clause of the First Amendment applicable as a prohibition against the States." 333 U. S., at 211. The Court, with Mr. Justice Reed alone dissenting, was unable to "accept either of these contentions." *Ibid.* Mr. Justice Frankfurter, joined by Justices Jackson, Rutledge and Burton, wrote a very comprehensive and scholarly concurrence in which he said that "[s]eparation is a requirement to abstain from fusing functions of government and of religious sects, not merely to treat them all equally." *Id.*, at 227. Continuing, he stated that:

> "the Constitution . . . prohibited the government common to all from becoming embroiled, however innocently, in the destructive religious conflicts of which the history of even this country records some dark pages." *Id.*, at 228.

In 1952 in *Zorach* v. *Clauson, supra,* MR. JUSTICE DOUGLAS for the Court reiterated:

> "There cannot be the slightest doubt that the First Amendment reflects the philosophy that Church and State should be separated. And so far as interference with the 'free exercise' of religion and an 'establishment' of religion are concerned, the separation must be complete and unequivocal. The First Amendment within the scope of its coverage permits no exception; the prohibition is absolute. The First Amendment, however, does not say that in every and all respects there shall be a separation of Church and State. Rather, it studiously defines the manner, the specific ways, in which there shall be no concert or union or dependency one on the other. That is the common sense of the matter." 343 U. S., at 312.

And then in 1961 in *McGowan* v. *Maryland* and in *Torcaso* v. *Watkins* each of these cases was discussed and approved. CHIEF JUSTICE WARREN in *McGowan,* for a unanimous Court on this point, said:

> "But, the First Amendment, in its final form, did not simply bar a congressional enactment *establishing a church;* it forbade all laws *respecting an estab-*

> *lishment of religion.*   Thus this Court has given the
> Amendment a 'broad interpretation . . . in the light
> of its history and the evils it was designed forever to
> suppress. . . .' "   366 U. S., at 441–442.

And MR. JUSTICE BLACK for the Court in *Torcaso,* without dissent but with Justices Frankfurter and HARLAN
concurring in the result, used this language:

> "We repeat and again reaffirm that neither a State
> nor the Federal Government can constitutionally
> force a person 'to profess a belief or disbelief in any
> religion.'   Neither can constitutionally pass laws or
> impose requirements which aid all religions as against
> non-believers, and neither can aid those religions
> based on a belief in the existence of God as against
> those religions founded on different beliefs."   367
> U. S., at 495.

Finally, in *Engel* v. *Vitale,* only last year, these principles were so universally recognized that the Court without the citation of a single case and over the sole dissent
of MR. JUSTICE STEWART reaffirmed them.   The Court
found the 22-word prayer used in "New York's program of daily classroom invocation of God's blessings as
prescribed in the Regents' prayer . . . [to be] a religious activity."   370 U. S., at 424.   It held that "it is
no part of the business of government to compose official
prayers for any group of the American people to recite
as a part of a religious program carried on by the government."   *Id.,* at 425.   In discussing the reach of the
Establishment and Free Exercise Clauses of the First
Amendment the Court said:

> "Although these two clauses may in certain instances
> overlap, they forbid two quite different kinds of gov-
> ernmental encroachment upon religious freedom.
> The Establishment Clause, unlike the Free Exercise

Clause, does not depend upon any showing of direct governmental compulsion and is violated by the enactment of laws which establish an official religion whether those laws operate directly to coerce non-observing individuals or not. This is not to say, of course, that laws officially prescribing a particular form of religious worship do not involve coercion of such individuals. When the power, prestige and financial support of government is placed behind a particular religious belief, the indirect coercive pressure upon religious minorities to conform to the prevailing officially approved religion is plain." *Id.,* at 430–431.

And in further elaboration the Court found that the "first and most immediate purpose [of the Establishment Clause] rested on a belief that a union of government and religion tends to destroy government and to degrade religion." *Id.,* at 431. When government, the Court said, allies itself with one particular form of religion, the inevitable result is that it incurs "the hatred, disrespect and even contempt of those who held contrary beliefs." *Ibid.*

<h2 style="text-align:center">V.</h2>

The wholesome "neutrality" of which this Court's cases speak thus stems from a recognition of the teachings of history that powerful sects or groups might bring about a fusion of governmental and religious functions or a concert or dependency of one upon the other to the end that official support of the State or Federal Government would be placed behind the tenets of one or of all orthodoxies. This the Establishment Clause prohibits. And a further reason for neutrality is found in the Free Exercise Clause, which recognizes the value of religious training, teaching and observance and, more particularly, the right of every person to freely choose his own course with reference thereto, free of any compulsion from the state. This the Free Exercise Clause guarantees. Thus, as we have seen, the two clauses may overlap. As we have indicated, the Establishment Clause has been directly considered by this Court eight times in the past score of years and, with only one Justice dissenting on the point, it has consistently held that the clause withdrew all legislative power respecting religious belief or the expression thereof. The test may be stated as follows: what are the purpose and the primary effect of the enactment? If either is the advancement or inhibition of religion then the enactment exceeds the scope of legislative power as circumscribed by the Constitution. That is to say that to withstand the strictures of the Establishment Clause there must be a secular legislative purpose and a primary effect that neither advances nor inhibits religion. *Everson* v. *Board of Education, supra; McGowan* v. *Maryland, supra,* at 442. The Free Exercise Clause, likewise considered many times here, withdraws from legislative power, state and federal, the exertion of any restraint on the free exercise of religion. Its purpose is to secure religious liberty in the individual by prohibiting any invasions thereof by civil authority. Hence it is necessary in a free exercise case for one to show the coercive effect of the enactment as it operates against him in the practice of his religion. The distinction between the two clauses is apparent—a violation of the Free Exercise Clause is predicated on coercion while the Establishment Clause violation need not be so attended.

Applying the Establishment Clause principles to the cases at bar we find that the States are requiring the selection and reading at the opening of the school day of verses from the Holy Bible and the recitation of the Lord's Prayer by the students in unison. These exercises are prescribed as part of the curricular activities of students who are required by law to attend school. They are held in the school buildings under the supervision and with the participation of teachers employed in those schools. None of these factors, other than compulsory school attendance, was present in the program upheld in *Zorach* v. *Clauson.* The trial court in No. 142 has found that such an opening exercise is a religious ceremony and was intended by the State to be so. We agree with the trial court's finding is to the religious character of the exercises. Given that finding the exercises and the law requiring them are in violation of the Establishment Clause.

There is no such specific finding as to the religious character of the exercises in No. 119, and the State contends (as does the State in No. 142) that the program is an effort to extend its benefits to all public school children without regard to their religious belief. Included within its secular purposes, it says, are the promotion of moral values, the contradiction to the materialistic trends of our times, the perpetuation of our institutions and the teaching of literature. The case came up on demurrer, of course, to a petition which alleged that the uniform practice under the rule had been to read from the King James version of the Bible and that the exercise was sectarian. The short answer, therefore, is that the religious character of the exercise was admitted by the State. But even if its purpose is not strictly religious, it is sought to be accomplished through readings, without comment, from the Bible. Surely the place of the Bible as an instrument of religion cannot be gainsaid, and the State's recognition of the pervading religious character of the ceremony is evident from the rule's specific permission of the alternative use of the Catholic Douay version as well as the recent amendment permitting nonattendance at the exercises. None of these factors is consistent with the contention that the Bible is here used either as an instrument for nonreligious moral inspiration or as a reference for the teaching of secular subjects.

The conclusion follows that in both cases the laws require religious exercises and such exercises are being conducted in direct violation of the rights of the appellees and petitioners.[9] Nor are these required exercises mitigated by the fact that individual students may absent themselves upon parental request, for that fact furnishes no defense to a claim of unconstitutionality under the Establishment Clause. See *Engel* v. *Vitale, supra,* at 430. Further, it is no defense to urge that the religious practices here may be relatively minor encroachments on the First Amendment. The breach of neutrality that is today a trickling stream may all too soon become a raging torrent and, in the words of Madison, "it is proper to take alarm at the first experiment on our liberties." Memorial and Remonstrance Against Religious Assessments, quoted in *Everson, supra,* at 65.

It is insisted that unless these religious exercises are permitted a "religion of secularism" is established in the

---

[9] It goes without saying that the laws and practices involved here can be challenged only by persons having standing to complain. But the requirements for standing to challenge state action under the Establishment Clause, unlike those relating to the Free Exercise Clause, do not include proof that particular religious freedoms are infringed. *McGowan* v. *Maryland, supra,* at 429–430. The parties here are school children and their parents, who are directly affected by the laws and practices against which their complaints are directed. These interests surely suffice to give the parties standing to complain. See *Engle* v. *Vitale, supra.* Cf. *McCollum* v. *Board of Education, supra; Everson* v. *Board of Education, supra.* Compare *Doremus* v. *Board of Education,* 342 U. S. 429 (1952), which involved the same substantive issues presented here. The appeal was there dismissed upon the graduation of the school child involved and because of the appellants' failure to establish standing as taxpayers.

schools. We agree of course that the State may not establish a "religion of secularism" in the sense of affirmatively opposing or showing hostility to religion, thus "preferring those who believe in no religion over those who do believe." *Zorach* v. *Clauson, supra,* at 314. We do not agree, however, that this decision in any sense has that effect. In addition, it might well be said that one's education is not complete without a study of comparative religion or the history of religion and its relationship to the advancement of civilization. It certainly may be said that the Bible is worthy of study for its literary and historic qualities. Nothing we have said here indicates that such study of the Bible or of religion, when presented objectively as part of a secular program of education, may not be effected consistent with the First Amendment. But the exercises here do not fall into those categories. They are religious exercises, required by the States in violation of the command of the First Amendment that the Government maintain strict neutrality, neither aiding nor opposing religion.

Finally, we cannot accept that the concept of neutrality, which does not permit a State to require a religious exercise even with the consent of the majority of those affected, collides with the majority's right to free exercise of religion.[10] While the Free Exercise Clause clearly prohibits the use of state action to deny the rights of free exercise to *anyone,* it has never meant that a majority could use the machinery of the State to practice its beliefs. Such a contention was effectively answered by Mr.

---

[10] We are not of course presented with and therefore do not pass upon a situation such as military service, where the Government regulates the temporal and geographic environment of individuals to a point that, unless it permits voluntary religious services to be conducted with the use of government facilities, military personnel would be unable to engage in the practice of their faiths.

Justice Jackson for the Court in *West Virginia Board of Education* v. *Barnette,* 319 U. S. 624, 638 (1943):

> "The very purpose of a Bill of Rights was to withdraw certain subjects from the vicissitudes of political controversy, to place them beyond the reach of majorities and officials and to establish them as legal principles to be applied by the courts. One's right to . . . freedom of worship . . . and other fundamental rights may not be submitted to vote; they depend on the outcome of no elections."

The place of religion in our society is an exalted one, achieved through a long tradition of reliance on the home, the church and the inviolable citadel of the individual heart and mind. We have come to recognize through bitter experience that it is not within the power of government to invade that citadel, whether its purpose or effect be to aid or oppose, to advance or retard. In the relationship between man and religion, the State is firmly committed to a position of neutrality. Though the application of that rule requires interpretation of a delicate sort, the rule itself is clearly and concisely stated in the words of the First Amendment. Applying that rule to the facts of these cases, we affirm the judgment in No. 142. In No. 119, the judgment is reversed and the cause remanded to the Maryland Court of Appeals for further proceedings consistent with this opinion.

It is so ordered.

SUPREME COURT OF THE UNITED STATES

Nos. 142 AND 119.—OCTOBER TERM, 1962.

School District of Abington Township, Pennsylvania, et al., Appellants, 142 *v.* Edward Lewis Schempp et al.	On Appeal From the United States District Court for the Eastern District of Pennsylvania.
William J. Murray III, etc., et al., Petitioners, 119 *v.* John N. Curlett, President, et al., Individually, and Constituting the Board of School Commissioners of Baltimore City.	On Writ of Certiorari to the Court of Appeals of Maryland.

[June 17, 1963.]

MR. JUSTICE DOUGLAS, concurring.

I join the opinion of the Court and add a few words in explanation.

While the Free Exercise Clause of the First Amendment is written in terms of what the State may not require of the individual, the Establishment Clause, serving the same goal of individual religious freedom, is written in different terms.

Establishment of a religion can be achieved in several ways. The church and state can be one; the church may control the state or the state may control the church; or the relationship may take one of several possible forms of a working arrangement between the two bodies.[1] Under

---

[1] See Bates, Religious Liberty: An Inquiry (1945), 9–14, 239–252; Cobb, Religious Liberty in America (1902), 1–2, cc. IV, V; Gledhill, Pakistan, The Development of its Laws and Constitution (8 British

all of these arrangements the church typically has a place in the state's budget, and church law usually governs such matters as baptism, marriage, divorce and separation, at least for its members and sometimes for the entire body politic.[2] Education, too, is usually high on the priority list of church interests.[3] In the past schools were often made the exclusive responsibility of the church. Today in some state-church countries the state runs the public schools, but compulsory religious exercises are often required of some or all students. Thus, under the agreement Franco made with the Holy See when he came to power in Spain, "The Church regained its place in the national budget. It insists on baptising all children and has made the catechism obligatory in state schools." [4]

The vice of all such arrangements under the Establishment Clause is that the state is lending its assistance to a church's efforts to gain and keep adherents. Under the First Amendment it is strictly a matter for the individual and his church as to what church he will belong to and how much support, in the way of belief, time, activity or

Commonwealth, 1957), 11–15; Keller, Church and State on the European Continent (1936), c. 2; Pfeffer, Church, State, and Freedom (1953), c. 2; 1 Stokes, Church and State in the United States (1950), 151–169.

[2] See III Stokes, *op. cit., supra,* n. 1, 42–67; Bates, *op. cit., supra,* n. 1, 9–11, 58–59, 98, 245; Gledhill, *op. cit., supra,* n. 1, 128, 192, 205, 208; Rackman, Israel's Emerging Constitution (1955), 120–134; Drinan, Religious Freedom in Israel, America (Apr. 6, 1963), 456–457.

[3] See II Stokes, *op. cit., supra,* n. 1, 488–548; Boles, The Bible, Religion, and the Public Schools (2d ed. 1963), 4–10; Rackman, *op. cit., supra,* n. 2, at 136–141; O'Brien, The *Engel* Case From A Swiss Perspective, 61 Mich. L. Rev. 1069; Freund, Muslim Education in West Pakistan, 56 Religious Education 31.

[4] Bates, *op. cit., supra,* n. 1, at 18; Pfeffer, *op. cit., supra,* n. 1, at 28–31; Thomas, The Balance of Forces in Spain, 41 Foreign Affairs, 208, 210.

money, he will give to it. "This pure Religious Liberty" "declared . . . [all forms of church-state relationships] and their fundamental idea to be oppressions of conscience and abridgments of that liberty which God and nature had conferred on every living soul." [5]

In these cases we have no coercive religious exercise aimed at making the students conform. The prayers announced are not compulsory, though some may think they have that indirect effect because the nonconformist student may be induced to participate for fear of being called an "odd-ball." But that coercion, if it be present, has not been shown; so the vices of the present regimes are different.

These regimes violate the Establishment Clause in two different ways. In each case the State is conducting a religious exercise; and, as the Court holds, that cannot be done without violating the "neutrality" required of the State by the balance of power between individual, church and state that has been struck by the First Amendment. But the Establishment Clause is not limited to precluding the State itself from conducting religious exercises. It also forbids the State to employ its facilities or funds in a way that gives any church, or all churches, greater strength in our society than it would have by relying on its members alone. Thus, the present regimes must fall under that clause for the additional reason that public funds, though small in amount, are being used to promote a religious exercise. Through the mechanism of the State, all of the people are being required to finance a religious exercise that only some of the people want and that violates the sensibilities of others.

The most effective way to establish any institution is to finance it; and this truth is reflected in the appeals by

---

[5] Cobb, *op. cit., supra*, n. 1, at 2.

church groups for public funds to finance their religious schools.[6] Financing a church either in its strictly religious activities or in its other activities is equally unconstitutional, as I understand the Establishment Clause. Budgets for one activity may be technically separable from budgets for others.[7] But the institution is an inseparable whole, a living organism, which is strengthened in proselytizing when it is strengthened in any department by contributions from other than its own members.

Such contributions may not be made by the State even in a minor degree without violating the Establishment Clause. It is not the amount of public funds expended; as this case illustrates, it is the use to which public funds are put that is controlling. For the First Amendment does not say that some forms of establishment are allowed; it says that "no law respecting an establishment of religion" shall be made. What may not be done directly may not be done indirectly lest the Establishment Clause become a mockery.

---

[6] See II Stokes, *op. cit., supra,* n. 1, at 681–695.
[7] See Accountants' Handbook (4th ed. 1956) 4.8–4.15.

SUPREME COURT OF THE UNITED STATES

Nos. 142 AND 119.—OCTOBER TERM, 1962.

School District of Abington Township, Pennsylvania, et al., Appellants, 142 v. Edward Lewis Schempp et al.	On Appeal From the United States District Court for the Eastern District of Pennsylvania.
William J. Murray III, etc., et al., Petitioners, 119 v. John N. Curlett, President, et al., Individually, and Constituting the Board of School Commissioners of Baltimore City.	On Writ of Certiorari to the Court of Appeals of Maryland.

[June 17, 1963.]

MR. JUSTICE BRENNAN, concurring.

Almost a century and a half ago, John Marshall, in *M'Culloch* v. *Maryland,* enjoined: ". . . we must never forget, that it is *a constitution* we are expounding." 4 Wheat. 316, 407. The Court's historic duty to expound the meaning of the Constitution has encountered few issues more intricate or more demanding than that of the relationship between religion and the public schools. Since undoubtedly we are "a religious people whose institutions presuppose a Supreme Being," *Zorach* v. *Clauson,* 343 U. S. 306, 313, deep feelings are aroused when aspects of that relationship are claimed to violate the injunction of the First Amendment that government may make "no law respecting an establishment of religion, or prohibiting the free exercise thereof . . . ." Americans regard the public schools as a most vital civic institution for the preservation of a democratic system of government. It is therefore understandable that the constitutional prohibitions encounter their severest test when they are sought to be applied in the school classroom. Nevertheless it is this Court's inescapable duty to declare whether exercises in the public schools of the States, such as those of Pennsylvania and Maryland questioned here, are involvements of religion in public institutions of a kind which offends the First and Fourteenth Amendments.

When John Locke ventured in 1689, "I esteem it above all things necessary to distinguish exactly the business of civil government from that of religion and to settle the just bounds that lie between the one and the other," [1] he anticipated the necessity which would be thought by the Framers to require adoption of a First Amendment, but not the difficulty that would be experienced in defining those "just bounds." The fact is that the line which separates the secular from the sectarian in American life is elusive. The difficulty of defining the boundary with precision inheres in a paradox central to our scheme of liberty. While our institutions reflect a firm conviction that we are a religious people, those institutions by solemn constitutional injunction may not officially involve religion in such a way as to prefer, discriminate against, or oppress, a particular sect or religion. Equally the Constitution enjoins those involvements of religious with secular institutions which (a) serve the essentially religious activities of religious institutions; (b) employ the organs of government for essentially religious purposes; or (c) use essentially religious means to serve governmental ends where secular means would suffice. The constitutional mandate expresses a deliberate and considered judgment that such matters are to be left to the conscience of the citizen, and declares as a basic postulate of the relation

---

[1] Locke, A Letter Concerning Tolerance in 35 Great Books of the Western World (Hutchins ed. 1952), 2.

between the citizen and his government that "the rights of conscience are, in their nature, of peculiar delicacy, and will little bear the gentlest touch of governmental hand . . . ." [2]

I join fully in the opinion and the judgment of the Court. I see no escape from the conclusion that the exercises called in question in these two cases violate the constitutional mandate. The reasons we gave only last Term in *Engel* v. *Vitale,* 370 U. S. 421, for finding in the New York Regents' prayer an impermissible establishment of religion, compel the same judgment of the practices at bar. The involvement of the secular with the religious is no less intimate here; and it is constitutionally irrelevant that the State has not composed the material for the inspirational exercises presently involved. It should be unnecessary to observe that our holding does not declare that the First Amendment manifests hostility to the practice or teaching of religion, but only applies prohibitions incorporated in the Bill of Rights in recognition of historic needs shared by Church and State alike. While it is my view that not every involvement of religion in public life is unconstitutional, I consider the exercises at bar a form of involvement which clearly violates the Establishment Clause.

The importance of the issue and the deep conviction with which views on both sides are held seem to me to justify detailing at some length my reasons for joining the Court's judgment and opinion.

I.

The First Amendment forbids both the abridgment of the free exercise of religion and the enactment of laws "respecting an establishment of religion." The two

---

[2] Representative Daniel Carroll of Maryland during debate upon the proposed Bill of Rights in the First Congress, August 15, 1789, I Annals of Cong. 730.

clauses, although distinct in their objectives and their applicability, emerged together from a common panorama of history. The inclusion of both restraints upon the power of Congress to legislate concerning religious matters shows unmistakably that the Framers of the First Amendment were not content to rest the protection of religious liberty exclusively upon either clause. "In assuring the free exercise of religion," Mr. Justice Frankfurter has said, "the Framers of the First Amendment were sensitive to the then recent history of those persecutions and impositions of civil disability with which sectarian majorities in virtually all of the Colonies had visited deviation in the matter of conscience. This protection of unpopular creeds, however, was not to be the full extent of the Amendment's guarantee of freedom from governmental intrusion in matters of faith. The battle in Virginia, hardly four years won, where James Madison had led the forces of disestablishment in successful opposition to Patrick Henry's proposed Assessment Bill levying a general tax for the support of Christian teachers, was a vital and compelling memory in 1789." *McGowan* v. *Maryland*, 366 U. S. 420, 464–465.

It is true that the Framers' immediate concern was to prevent the setting up of an official federal church of the kind which England and some of the Colonies had long supported. But nothing in the text of the Establishment Clause supports the view that the prevention of the setting up of an official church was meant to be the full extent of the prohibitions against official involvements in religion. It has rightly been said:

> "If the framers of the Amendment meant to prohibit Congress merely from the establishment of a 'church,' one might properly wonder why they didn't so state. That the words *church* and *religion* were regarded as synonymous seems highly improbable,

> particularly in view of the fact that the contemporary
> state constitutional provisions dealing with the sub-
> ject of establishment used definite phrases such as
> 'religious sect,' 'sect,' or 'denomination.' . . . With
> such specific wording in contemporary state consti-
> tutions, why was not a similar wording adopted for
> the First Amendment if its framers intended to pro-
> hibit nothing more than the States were prohibit-
> ing?" Lardner, How Far Does the Constitution
> Separate Church and State?, 45 Am. Pol. Sci. Rev.
> 110, 112 (1951).

Plainly, the Establishment Clause, in the contempla-
tion of the Framers, "did not limit the constitutional
proscription to any particular, dated form of state-
supported theological venture." "What Virginia had
long practiced, and what Madison, Jefferson and others
fought to end, was the extension of civil government's
support to religion in a manner which made the two in
some degree interdependent, and thus threatened the
freedom of each. The purpose of the Establishment
Clause was to assure that the national legislature would
not exert its power in the service of any purely religious
end; that it would not, as Virginia and virtually all of
the Colonies had done, make of religion, as religion, an
object of legislation. . . . The Establishment Clause
withdrew from the sphere of legitimate legislative concern and competence a specific, but comprehensive, area
of human conduct: man's belief or disbelief in the verity
of some transcendental idea and man's expression in
action of that belief or disbelief." *McGowan* v. *Maryland, supra,* at 465–466 (opinion of Frankfurter, J.).

In sum, the history which our prior decisions have
summoned to aid interpretation of the Establishment
Clause permits little doubt that its prohibition was
designed comprehensively to prevent those official in-

volvements of religion which would tend to foster or discourage religious worship or belief.

But an awareness of history and an appreciation of the aims of the Founding Fathers do not always resolve concrete problems. The specific question before us has, for example, aroused vigorous dispute whether the architects of the First Amendment—James Madison and Thomas Jefferson particularly—understood the prohibition against any "law respecting an establishment of religion" to reach devotional exercises in the public schools.[3] It may be that Jefferson and Madison would have held such exercises to be permissible—although even in Jefferson's case serious doubt is suggested by his admonition against "putting the Bible and Testament into the hands of the children at an age when their judgments are not sufficiently matured for religious inquiries . . . ."[4] But

---

[3] See Healey, Jefferson on Religion in Public Education (1962); Boles, The Bible, Religion, and the Public Schools (1961), 16–21; Butts, The American Tradition in Religion and Education (1950), 119–130; Cahn, On Government and Prayer, 37 N. Y. U. L. Rev. 981 (1962); Costanzo, Thomas Jefferson, Religious Education and Public Law, 8 J. Pub. Law 81 (1959); Comment, The Supreme Court, the First Amendment, and Religion in the Public Schools, 63 Col. L. Rev. 73, 79–83 (1963).

[4] Jefferson's caveat was in full:

"Instead, therefore, of putting the Bible and Testament into the hands of the children at an age when their judgments are not sufficiently matured for religious inquiries, their memories may here be stored with the most useful facts from Grecian, Roman, European and American history." 2 Writings of Thomas Jefferson (Memorial ed. 1903), 204.

Compare Jefferson's letter to his nephew, Peter Carr, when the latter was about to begin the study of law, in which Jefferson outlined a suggested course of private study of religion since "[y]our reason is now mature enough to examine this object." Letter to Peter Carr, August 10, 1787, in Padover, The Complete Jefferson (1943), 1058. Jefferson seems to have opposed sectarian instruction at any level of public education, see Healey, Jefferson on Religion in Public

I doubt that their view, even if perfectly clear one way or
the other, would supply a dispositive answer to the question presented by these cases. A more fruitful inquiry,
it seems to me, is whether the practices here challenged
threaten those consequences which the Framers deeply
feared; whether, in short, they tend to promote that type
of interdependence between religion and state which the
First Amendment was designed to prevent.[5] Our task is

Education (1962), 206–210, 256, 264–265. The absence of any mention of religious instruction in the projected elementary and secondary schools contrasts significantly with Jefferson's quite explicit proposals concerning religious instruction at the University of Virginia.
His draft for "A Bill for the More General Diffusion of Knowledge"
in 1779, for example, outlined in some detail the secular curriculum
for the public schools, while avoiding any references to religious
studies. See Padover, *supra*, at 1048–1054. The later draft of an
"Act for Establishing Elementary Schools" which Jefferson submitted
to the Virginia General Assembly in 1817 provided that "no religious
reading, instruction or exercise, shall be prescribed or practiced inconsistent with the tenets of any religious sect or denomination." Padover, *supra*, at 1076. Reliance upon Jefferson's apparent willingness
to permit certain religious instruction at the University seems, therefore, to lend little support to such instruction in the elementary and
secondary schools. Compare, *e. g.*, Corwin, A Constitution of Powers
in a Secular State (1951), 104–106; Costanzo, Thomas Jefferson,
Religious Education and Public Law, 8 J. Pub. Law 81, 100–106
(1959).

[5] Cf. Mr. Justice Rutledge's observations in *Everson* v. *Board of
Education,* 330 U. S. 1, 53–54 (dissenting opinion). See also Fellman,
Separation of Church and State in the United States: A Summary
View, 1950 Wis. L. Rev. 427, 428–429; Rosenfield, Separation of
Church and State in the Public Schools, 22 U. of Pitt. L. Rev.
561, 569 (1961); MacKinnon, Freedom?—or Toleration?, The Problem of Church and State in the United States, [1959] Pub. Law
374. One author has suggested these reasons for cautious application
of the history of the Constitution's religious guarantees to contemporary problems:

"First, the brevity of Congressional debate and the lack of writings
on the question by the framers make any historical argument incon-

to translate "the majestic generalities of the Bill of Rights, conceived as part of the pattern of liberal government in the eighteenth century, into concrete restraints on officials dealing with the problems of the twentieth century . . . ." *West Virginia State Board of Education* v. *Barnette,* 319 U. S. 624, 639.

A too literal quest for the advice of the Founding Fathers upon the issues of these cases seems to me futile and misdirected for several reasons: First, on our precise problem the historical record is at best ambiguous, and statements can readily be found to support either side of the proposition. The ambiguity of history is understandable if we recall the nature of the problems uppermost in the thinking of the statesmen who fashioned the religious guarantees; they were concerned with far more flagrant intrusions of government into the realm of religion than any that our century has witnessed.[6] While it is

---

clusive and open to serious question. Second, the amendment was designed to outlaw practices which had existed before its writing, but there is no authoritative declaration of the specific practices at which it was aimed. And third, most of the modern religious-freedom cases turn on issues which were at most academic in 1789 and perhaps did not exist at all. Public education was almost nonexistent in 1789, and the question of religious education in public schools may not have been foreseen." Beth, The American Theory of Church and State (1958), 88.

[6] See generally, for discussion of the early efforts for disestablishment of the established colonial churches, and of the conditions against which the proponents of separation of church and state contended, Sweet, The Story of Religion in America (1950), c. XIII; Cobb, The Rise of Religious Liberty in America (1902), c. IX; Eckenrode, Separation of Church and State in Virginia (1910); Brant, James Madison—The Nationalist, 1780–1787 (1948), c. XXII; Bowers, The Young Jefferson (1945), 193–199; Butts, The American Tradition in Church and State (1950), c. II; Kruse, The Historical Meaning and Judicial Construction of the Establishment of Religion Clause of the First Amendment, 2 Washburn L. J. 65, 79–83 (1962). Compare also Alexander Hamilton's conception of "the characteristic difference between a tolerated and established religion" and his

clear to me that the Framers meant the Establishment Clause to prohibit more than the creation of an established federal church such as existed in England, I have no doubt that, in their preoccupation with the imminent question of established churches, they gave no distinct consideration to the particular question whether the clause also forbade devotional exercises in public institutions.

Second, the structure of American education has greatly changed since the First Amendment was adopted. In the context of our modern emphasis upon public education available to all citizens, any views of the eighteenth century as to whether the exercises at bar are an "establishment" offer little aid to decision. Education, as the Framers knew it, was in the main confined to private schools more often than not under strictly sectarian supervision. Only gradually did control of education pass largely to public officials.[7] It would, therefore,

___

grounds of opposition to the latter, in his remarks on the Quebec Bill in 1775, 2 Works of Alexander Hamilton (Hamilton ed. 1850), 133–138. Compare, for the view that contemporary evidence reveals a design of the Framers to forbid not only formal establishment of churches, but various forms of incidental aid to or support of religion, Lardner, How Far Does the Constitution Separate Church and State?, 45 Am. Pol. Sci. Rev. 110, 112–115 (1951).

[7] The origins of the modern movement for free state-supported education cannot be fixed with precision. In England, the Levellers unavailingly urged in their platform of 1649 the establishment of free primary education for all, or at least for boys. See Brailsford, The Levellers and the English Revolution (1961), 534. In the North American Colonies, education was almost without exception under private sponsorship and supervision, frequently in control of the dominant Protestant sects. This condition prevailed after the Revolution and into the first quarter of the nineteenth century. See generally Mason, Moral Values and Secular Education (1950), c. II; Thayer, The Role of the School in American Society (1960), c. X; Greene, Religion and the State: The Making and Testing of an American Tradition (1941), 120–122. Thus, Virginia's colonial Governor Berkeley exclaimed in 1671: "I thank God there are no free schools nor printing, and I hope we shall not have them these hundred

hardly be significant if the fact was that the nearly universal devotional exercises in the schools of the young
Republic did not provoke criticism; even today religious
ceremonies in church-supported private schools are constitutionally unobjectionable.

---

years; for learning has brought disobedience, and heresy, and sects
into the world . . . ." (Emphasis deleted.) Bates, Religious Liberty: An Inquiry (1945), 327.

The exclusively private control of American education did not,
however, quite survive Berkeley's expectations. Benjamin Franklin's
proposals in 1749 for a Philadelphia Academy heralded the dawn
of publicly supported secondary education, although the proposal
did not bear immediate fruit. See Johnson and Yost, Separation of
Church and State in the United States (1948), 26–27. Jefferson's
elaborate plans for a public school system in Virginia came to naught
after the defeat in 1796 of his proposed Elementary School Bill, which
found little favor among the wealthier legislators. See Bowers, The
Young Jefferson (1945), 182–186. It was not until the 1820's and
1830's, under the impetus of Jacksonian democracy, that a system
of public education really took root in the United States. See 1 Beard,
The Rise of American Civilization (1937), 810–818. One force behind
the development of secular public schools may have been a growing
dissatisfaction with the tightly sectarian control over private education, see Harner, Religion's Place in General Education (1949), 29–30.
Yet the burgeoning public school systems did not immediately sup-
plant the old sectarian and private institutions; Alexis de Tocqueville,
for example, remarked after his tour of the Eastern States in 1831
that "[a]lmost all education is entrusted to the clergy." 1 Democracy in America (Bradley ed. 1945) 309, n. 4. And compare Lord
Bryce's observations, a half century later, on the still largely denominational character of American higher education, 2 The American
Commonwealth (1933), 734–735.

Efforts to keep the public schools of the early nineteenth century
free from sectarian influence were of two kinds. One took the form
of constitutional provisions and statutes adopted by a number of
States forbidding appropriations from the public treasury for the
support of religious instruction in any manner. See Moehlman, The
Wall of Separation Between Church and State (1951), 132–135;
Lardner, How Far Does the Constitution Separate Church and State?,
45 Am. Pol. Sci. Rev. 110, 122 (1951). The other took the form

Third, our religious composition makes us a vastly more diverse people than were our forefathers. They knew differences chiefly among Protestant sects. Today the Nation is far more heterogenous religiously, including as it does substantial minorities not only of Catholics and

---

of measures directed against the use of sectarian reading and teaching materials in the schools. The texts used in the earliest public schools had been largely taken over from the private academies, and retained a strongly religious character and content. See Nichols, Religion and American Democracy (1959), 64–80; Kinney, Church and State, The Struggle for Separation in New Hampshire, 1630–1900 (1955), 150–153. In 1827, however, Massachusetts enacted a statute providing that school boards might not thereafter "direct any school books to be purchased or used in any of the schools . . . which are calculated to favor any particular religious sect or tenet." 2 Stokes, Church and State in the United States (1950), 53. For further discussion of the background of the Massachusetts law and difficulties in its early application, see Dunn, What Happened to Religious Education? (1958), c. IV. As other States followed the example of Massachusetts, the use of sectarian texts was in time as widely prohibited as the appropriation of public funds for religious instruction.

Concerning the evolution of the American public school systems free of sectarian influence, compare Mr. Justice Frankfurter's account:

"It is pertinent to remind that the establishment of this principle of Separation in the field of education was not due to any decline in the religious beliefs of the people. Horace Mann was a devout Christian, and the deep religious feeling of James Madison is stamped upon the Remonstrance. The secular public school did not imply indifference to the basic role of religion in the life of the people, nor rejection of religious education as a means of fostering it. The claims of religion were not minimized by refusing to make the public schools agencies for their assertion. The non-sectarian or secular public school was the means of reconciling freedom in general with religious freedom. The sharp confinement of the public schools to secular education was a recognition of the need of a democratic society to educate its children, insofar as the State undertook to do so, in an atmosphere free from pressures in a realm in which pressures are most resisted and where conflicts are most easily and most bitterly engendered." *Illinois ex rel. McCollum* v. *Board of Education,* 333 U. S. 203, 216.

Jews but as well of those who worship according to no version of the Bible and those who worship no God at all.[8] See *Torcaso* v. *Watkins*, 367 U. S. 488, 495. In the face of such profound changes, practices which may have been objectionable to no one in the time of Jefferson and Madison may today be highly offensive to many persons, the deeply devout and the nonbelievers alike.

Whatever Jefferson or Madison would have thought of Bible reading or the recital of the Lord's Prayer in what few public schools existed in their day, our use of the history of their time must limit itself to broad purposes, not specific practices. By such a standard, I am persuaded, as is the Court, that the devotional exercises carried on in the Baltimore and Abington schools offend the First Amendment because they sufficiently threaten in our day those substantive evils the fear of which called forth the Establishment Clause of the First Amendment. It is "*a constitution* we are expounding," and our interpretation of the First Amendment must necessarily be responsive to the much more highly charged nature of religious questions in contemporary society.

Fourth, the American experiment in free public education available to all children has been guided in large measure by the dramatic evolution of the religious diver-

---

[8] The comparative religious homogeneity of the United States at the time the Bill of Rights was adopted has been considered in Haller, The Puritan Background of the First Amendment, in Read, ed., The Constitution Reconsidered (1938), 131, 133–134; Beth, The American Theory of Church and State (1958), 74; Kinney, Church and State, The Struggle for Separation in New Hampshire, 1630–1900 (1955), 155–161. However, Madison suggested in the Fifty-first Federalist that the religious diversity which existed at the time of the Constitutional Convention constituted a source of strength for religious freedom, much as the multiplicity of economic and political interests enhanced the security of other civil rights. The Federalist (Cooke ed. 1961), 351–352.

sity among the population which our public schools serve. The interaction of these two important forces in our national life has placed in bold relief certain positive values in the consistent application to public institutions generally, and public schools particularly, of the constitutional decree against official involvements of religion which might produce the evils the Framers meant the Establishment Clause to forestall. The public schools are supported entirely, in most communities, by public funds—funds exacted not only from parents, nor alone from those who hold particular religious views, nor indeed from those who subscribe to any creed at all. It is implicit in the history and character of American public education that the public schools serve a uniquely *public* function: the training of American citizens in an atmosphere free of parochial, divisive, or separatist influences of any sort—an atmosphere in which children may assimilate a heritage common to all American groups and religions. See *Illinois ex rel. McCollum* v. *Board of Education,* 333 U. S. 203. This is a heritage neither theistic nor atheistic, but simply civic and patriotic. See *Meyer* v. *Nebraska,* 262 U. S. 390, 400–403.

Attendance at the public schools has never been compulsory; parents remain morally and constitutionally free to choose the academic environment in which they wish their children to be educated. The relationship of the Establishment Clause of the First Amendment to the public school system is preeminently that of reserving such a choice to the individual parent, rather than vesting it in the majority of voters of each State or school district. The choice which is thus preserved is between a public secular education with its uniquely democratic values, and some form of private, or sectarian education, which offers values of its own. In my judgment the First Amendment forbids the State to inhibit that freedom of choice by diminishing the attractiveness of either alternative—either by restricting the liberty of the private schools to inculcate whatever values they wish, or by jeopardizing the freedom of the public school from private or sectarian pressures. The choice between these very different forms of education is one—very much like the choice of whether or not to worship—which our Constitution leaves to the individual parent. It is no proper function of the state or local government to influence or restrict that election. The lesson of history— drawn more from the experiences of other countries than from our own—is that a system of free public education forfeits its unique contribution to the growth of democratic citizenship when that choice ceases to be freely available to each parent.

II.

The exposition by this Court of the religious guarantees of the First Amendment has consistently reflected and reaffirmed the concerns which impelled the Framers to write those guarantees into the Constitution. It would be neither possible nor appropriate to review here the entire course of our decisions on religious questions. There emerge from those decisions, however, three principles of particular relevance to the issue presented by the cases at bar, and some attention to those decisions is therefore appropriate.

First. One line of decisions derives from contests for control of a church property or other internal ecclesiastical disputes. This line has settled the proposition that in order to give effect to the First Amendment's purpose of requiring on the part of all organs of government a strict neutrality toward theological questions, courts should not undertake to decide such questions. These principles were first expounded in the case of *Watson* v. *Jones*, 13

Wall. 679, which declared that judicial intervention in such a controversy would open up "the whole subject of the doctrinal theology, the usages and customs, the written laws, and fundamental organization of every religious denomination . . . ." 13 Wall., at 733. Courts above all must be neutral, for "[t]he law knows no heresy, and is committed to the support of no dogma, the establishment of no sect." [9] 13 Wall., at 728. This principle has recently been reaffirmed in *Kedroff* v. *St. Nicholas Cathe-*

---

[9] See Comment, The Power of Courts Over the Internal Affairs of Religious Groups, 43 Calif. L. Rev. 322 (1955); Comment, Judicial Intervention in Disputes Within Independent Church Bodies, 54 Mich. L. Rev. 102 (1955); Note, Judicial Intervention in Disputes Over the Use of Church Property, 75 Harv. L. Rev. 1142 (1962). Compare *Vidal* v. *Girard's Executors,* 2 How. 127. The principle of judicial nonintervention in essentially religious disputes appears to have been reflected in the decisions of several state courts declining to enforce essentially private agreements concerning the religious education and worship of children of separated or divorced parents. See, *e. g., Hackett* v. *Hackett,* 78 Ohio Abs. 485, 150 N. E. 2d 431; *Stanton* v. *Stanton,* 213 Ga. 545, 100 S. E. 2d 289; Friedman, The Parental Right to Control the Religious Education of a Child, 29 Harv. L. Rev. 485 (1916); 72 Harv. L. Rev. 372 (1958); Note, 10 West. Res. L. Rev. 171 (1959).

Governmental nonintervention in religious affairs and institutions seems assured by Article 26 of the Constitution of India, which provides:

"Subject to public order, morality and health, every religious denomination or any sect thereof shall have the right—

"(a) to establish and maintain institutions for religious and charitable purposes;

"(b) to manage its own affairs in matters of religion;

"(c) to own and acquire movable and immovable property; and

"(d) to administer such property in accordance with law." See 1 Chaudhri, Constitutional Rights and Limitations (1955), 875. This Article does not, however, appear to have completely foreclosed judicial inquiry into the merits of intradenominational disputes. See Gledhill, Fundamental Rights in India (1955), 101–102.

dral, 344 U. S. 94; and *Kreshik* v. *St. Nicholas Cathedral,* 363 U. S. 190.

The mandate of judicial neutrality in theological controversies met its severest test in *United States* v. *Ballard,* 322 U. S. 78. That decision put in sharp relief certain principles which bear directly upon the questions presented in these cases. Ballard was indicted for fraudulent use of the mails in the dissemination of religious literature. He requested that the trial court submit to the jury the question of the truthfulness of the religious views he championed. The requested charge was refused, and we upheld that refusal, reasoning that the First Amendment foreclosed any judicial inquiry into the truth or falsity of the defendant's religious beliefs. We said: "Man's relation to his God was made no concern of the state. He was granted the right to worship as he pleased and to answer to no man for the verity of his religious views." "Men may believe what they cannot prove. They may not be put to the proof of their religious doctrines or beliefs. . . . Many take their gospel from the New Testament. But it would hardly be supposed that they could be tried before a jury charged with the duty of determining whether those teachings contained false representations." 322 U. S., at 86–87.

The dilemma presented by the case was severe. While the alleged truthfulness of *nonreligious* publications could ordinarily have been submitted to the jury, Ballard was deprived of that defense only because the First Amendment forbids governmental inquiry into the verity of *religious* beliefs. In dissent Mr. Justice Jackson expressed the concern that under this construction of the First Amendment "[p]rosecutions of this character easily could degenerate into religious persecution." 322 U. S., at 95. The case shows how elusive is the line which enforces the Amendment's injunction of strict neutrality, while manifesting no official hostility toward religion—a line which must be considered in the cases now before us.[10] Some might view the result of the *Ballard* case as a manifestation of hostility—in that the conviction stood because the defense could not be raised. To others it might represent merely strict adherence to the principle of neutrality already expounded in the cases involving doctrinal disputes. Inevitably, insistence upon neutrality, vital as it surely is for untrammelled religious liberty, may appear to border upon religious hostility. But in the long view the independence of both church and state in their respective spheres will be better served by close adherence to the neutrality principle. If the choice is often difficult, the difficulty is endemic to issues implicating the religious guarantees of the First Amendment. Freedom of religion will be seriously jeopardized if we admit exceptions for no better reason than the difficulty of delineating hostility from neutrality in the closest cases.

---

[10] For a discussion of the difficulties inherent in the *Ballard* case, see Kurland, Religion and the Law (1962), 75–79. This Court eventually reversed the convictions on the quite unrelated ground that women had been systematically excluded from the jury, *Ballard* v. *United States,* 329 U. S. 187. For discussions of the difficulties in interpreting and applying the First Amendment so as to foster the objective of neutrality without hostility, see, *e. g.,* Katz, Freedom of Religion and State Neutrality, 20 U. of Chi. L. Rev. 426, 438 (1953); Kauper, Church, State and Freedom: A Review, 52 Mich. L. Rev. 829, 842 (1954). Compare, for an interesting apparent attempt to avoid the *Ballard* problem at the international level, Article 3 of the Multilateral Treaty between the United States and certain American Republics, which provides that extradition will not be granted, *inter alia,* when "the offense is . . . directed against religion." Blakely, American State Papers and Related Documents on Freedom in Religion (4th rev. ed. 1949), 316.

Second. It is only recently that our decisions have dealt with the question whether issues arising under the Establishment Clause may be isolated from problems implicating the Free Exercise Clause. *Everson* v. *Board of Education,* 330 U. S. 1, is in my view the first of our decisions which treats a problem of asserted unconstitutional involvement as raising questions purely under the Establishment Clause. A scrutiny of several earlier decisions said by some to have etched the contours of the clause shows that such cases neither raised nor decided any constitutional issues under the First Amendment. *Bradfield* v. *Roberts,* 175 U. S. 291, for example, involved challenges to a federal grant to a hospital administered by a Roman Catholic order. The Court rejected the claim for lack of evidence that any sectarian influence changed its character as a secular institution chartered as such by the Congress.[11]

Quick Bear v. *Leupp,* 210 U. S. 50, is also illustrative. The immediate question there was one of statutory construction, although the issue had originally involved the constitutionality of the use of federal funds to support sectarian education on Indian reservations. Congress had already prohibited federal grants for that purpose, thereby removing the broader issue, leaving only the question whether the statute authorized the appropriation for religious teaching of Treaty funds held by the Government in trust for the Indians. Since these were the Indians' own funds, the Court held only that the Indians might direct their use for such educational purposes as they chose, and that the administration by the Treasury of the disbursement of the funds did not inject into the case any issue of the propriety of the use of fed-

----

[11] See Kurland, Religion and the Law (1962), 32–34.

eral moneys.[12]   Indeed, the Court expressly approved the
reasoning of the Court of Appeals that to deny the
Indians the right to spend their own moneys for religious
purposes of their choice might well infringe the free exercise of their religion: "it seems inconceivable that Congress should have intended to prohibit them from receiving religious education at their own cost if they so desired
it . . . ."   210 U. S., at 82.   This case forecast, however,
an increasingly troublesome First Amendment paradox:
that the logical interrelationship between the establishment and free exercise clauses may produce situations
where an injunction against an apparent establishment
must be withheld in order to avoid infringement of rights
of free exercise.   That paradox was not squarely presented in *Quick Bear,* but the care taken by the Court
to avoid a constitutional confrontation discloses an awareness of possible conflicts between the two clauses.   I
shall come back to this problem later, *infra,* p. 67–71.

A third case in this group is *Cochran* v. *Louisiana State
Board,* 281 U. S. 370, which involved a challenge to a
state statute providing public funds to support a loan of
free text books to pupils of both public and private
schools.   The constitutional issues in this Court extended
no further than the claim that this program amounted to a
taking of private property for nonpublic use.   The Court
rejected the claim on the ground that no private use of

---

[12] Compare the treatment of an apparently very similar problem
in Article 28 of the Constitution of India:

"(1) No religious instruction shall be provided in any educational
institution wholly maintained out of State funds.

"(2) Nothing in clause (1) shall apply to an educational institution which is administered by the State but has been established
under any endowment or trust which requires that religious instruction shall be imparted in such institution."   1 Chaudhri, Constitutional Rights and Limitations (1955), 875–876, 939.

property was involved; ". . . we can not doubt that the taxing power of the State is exerted for a public purpose." 281 U. S., at 375. The case therefore raised no issue under the First Amendment.[13]

In *Pierce* v. *Society of Sisters,* 268 U. S. 510, a Catholic parochial school and a private but nonsectarian military academy challenged a state law requiring all children between certain ages to attend the public schools. This Court held the law invalid as an arbitrary and unreasonable interference both with the rights of the schools and with the liberty of the parents of the children who attended them. The due process guarantee of the Fourteenth Amendment "excludes any general power of the State to standardize its children by forcing them to accept instruction from public teachers only." 268 U. S., at 535. While one of the plaintiffs was indeed a parochial school, the case obviously decided no First Amendment question but recognized only the constitutional right to establish and patronize private schools—including parochial schools—which meet the state's reasonable minimum curricular requirements.

Third. It is true, as the Court says, that the "two clauses [Establishment and Free Exercise] may overlap." Because of the overlap, however, our decisions under the Free Exercise Clause bear considerable relevance to the problem now before us, and should be briefly reviewed. The early free exercise cases generally involved the objections of religious minorities to the application to them of general nonreligious legislation governing conduct. *Reynolds* v. *United States,* 98 U. S. 145, involved the claim that a belief in the sanctity of plural marriage pre-

---

[13] See Kurland, Religion and the Law (1962), 28–31; Fellman, Separation of Church and State in the United States: A Summary View, 1950 Wis. L. Rev. 427, 442.

cluded the conviction of members of a particular sect under nondiscriminatory legislation against such marriage. The Court rejected the claim, saying:

> "Laws are made for the government of actions, and while they cannot interfere with mere religious beliefs and opinions, they may with practices. . . . Can a man excuse his practices to the contrary because of his religious belief? To permit this would be to make the professed doctrines of religious belief superior to the law of the land, and in effect to permit every citizen to become a law unto himself. Government could exist only in name under such circumstances." [14]   98 U. S., at 166–167.

---

[14] This distinction, implicit in the First Amendment, had been made explicit in the original Virginia Bill of Rights provision that "all men are equally entitled to the free exercise of religion, according to the dictates of conscience, unpunished and unrestrained by the magistrates, unless, under color of religion, any man disturb the peace and happiness or safety of society." See Cobb, The Rise of Religious Liberty in America (1902), 491. Concerning various legislative limitations and restraints upon religiously motivated behavior which endangers or offends society, see Manwaring, Render Unto Caesar: The Flag-Salute Controversy (1962), 41–52. Various courts have applied this principle to proscribe certain religious exercises or activities which were thought to threaten the safety or morals of the participants or the rest of the community, *e. g., State* v. *Massey,* 229 N. C. 734, 51 S. E. 2d 179; *Harden* v. *State,* 188 Tenn. 17, 216 S. W. 708; *Lawson* v. *Commonwealth,* 291 Ky. 437, 164 S. W. 2d 972; cf. *Sweeney* v. *Webb,* 33 Tex. Civ. App. 324, 76 S. W. 766.

That the principle of these cases, and the distinction between belief and behavior, are susceptible of perverse application, may be suggested by Oliver Cromwell's mandate to the besieged Catholic community in Ireland:

"As to freedom of conscience, I meddle with no man's conscience; but if you mean by that, liberty to celebrate the Mass, I would have you understand that in no place where the power of the Parliament of England prevails shall that be permitted." Quoted in Hook, The Paradoxes of Freedom (1962), 23.

Davis v. *Beason,* 133 U. S. 333, similarly involved the claim that the First Amendment insulated from civil punishment certain practices inspired or motivated by religious beliefs. The claim was easily rejected: "It was never intended or supposed that the amendment could be invoked as a protection against legislation for the punishment of acts inimical to the peace, good order and morals of society." 133 U. S., at 342. See also *Mormon Church* v. *United States,* 136 U. S. 1; *Jacobson* v. *Massachusetts,* 197 U. S. 11; *Prince* v. *Massachusetts,* 321 U. S. 158; *Cleveland* v. *United States,* 329 U. S. 14.

But we must not confuse the issue of governmental power to regulate or prohibit conduct *motivated by religious beliefs* with the quite different problem of governmental authority to compel behavior *offensive to religious principles.* In *Hamilton* v. *Regents of the University of California,* 293 U. S. 245, the question was that of the power of a State to compel students at the State University to participate in military training instruction against their religious convictions. The validity of the statute was sustained against claims based upon the First Amendment. But the decision rested on a very narrow principle: since there was neither a constitutional right nor a legal obligation to attend the State University, the obligation to participate in military training courses, reflecting a legitimate state interest, might properly be imposed upon those who chose to attend. Although the rights protected by the First and Fourteenth Amendments were presumed to include "the right to entertain the beliefs, to adhere to the principles and to teach the doctrines on which these students base their objections to the order prescribing military training," those Amendments were construed not to free such students from the military training obligations if they chose to attend the University. Justices Brandeis, Cardozo and Stone, concurring separately, agreed that the requirement infringed no constitutionally protected liberties. They added, however, that the case presented no question under the Establishment Clause. The military instruction program was not an establishment since it in no way involved "instruction in the practice or tenets of a religion." 293 U. S., at 266. Since the only question was one of free exercise, they concluded, like the majority, that the strong state interest in training a citizen militia justified the restraints imposed, at least so long as attendance at the University was voluntary.[15]

Hamilton has not been overruled, although *United States* v. *Schwimmer*, 279 U. S. 644, and *United States* v. *Macintosh*, 283 U. S. 605, upon which the Court, in *Hamilton* relied, have since been overruled by *Girouard* v. *United States*, 328 U. S. 61. But if *Hamilton* retains any vitality with respect to higher education, we recognized its inapplicability to cognate questions in the public primary and secondary schools when we held in *West Virginia Board of Education* v. *Barnette, supra,* that a State had no power to expel from public schools students who refused on religious grounds to comply with a daily flag salute requirement. Of course, such a requirement was no more a law "respecting an establishment of religion" than the California law compelling the college students to take military training. The *Barnette* plaintiffs, moreover, did not ask that the whole exercise be enjoined, but only that an excuse or exemption be provided for those students whose religious beliefs forbade them to participate in the ceremony. The key to the holding that such

---

[15] With respect to the decision in *Hamilton* v. *Regents*, compare two recent comments: Kurland, Religion and the Law (1962), 40; and French, Comment, Unconstitutional Conditions: An Analysis, 50 Geo. L. J. 234, 246 (1961).

a requirement abridged rights of free exercise lay in the fact that attendance at school was not voluntary but compulsory. The Court said:

> "This issue is not prejudiced by the Court's previous holding that where a State, without compelling attendance, extends college facilities to pupils who voluntarily enroll, it may prescribe military training as part of the course without offense to the Constitution. . . . *Hamilton* v. *Regents,* 293 U. S. 245. In the present case attendance is not optional." 319 U. S., at 631–632.

The *Barnette* decision made another significant point. The Court held that the State must make participation in the exercise voluntary for all students and not alone for those who found participation obnoxious on religious grounds. In short, there was simply no need to "inquire whether nonconformist beliefs will exempt from the duty to salute" because the Court found no state "power to make the salute a legal duty." 319 U. S., at 635.

The distinctions between *Hamilton* and *Barnette* are, I think, crucial to the resolution of the cases before us. The different results of those cases are attributable only in part to a difference in the strength of the particular state interests which the respective statutes were designed to serve. Far more significant is the fact that *Hamilton* dealt with the voluntary attendance at college of young adults, while *Barnette* involved the compelled attendance of young children at elementary and secondary schools.[16] This distinction warrants a difference in constitutional

---

[16] See generally as to the background and history of the *Barnette* case, Manwaring, Render Unto Caesar: The Flag-Salute Controversy (1962), especially at 252–253. Compare, for the interesting treatment of a problem similar to that of *Barnette,* in a nonconstitutional context, *Chabot* v. *Les Commissaires D'Ecoles de Lamorandière,* [1957] Que. B. R. 707, noted in 4 McGill L. J. 268 (1958).

results. And it is with the involuntary attendance of young school children that we are exclusively concerned in the cases now before the Court.

III.

No one questions that the Framers of the First Amendment intended to restrict exclusively the powers of the Federal Government.[17] Whatever limitations that Amendment now imposes upon the States derive from the Fourteenth Amendment. The process of absorption of the religious guarantees of the First Amendment as protections against the States under the Fourteenth Amendment began with the Free Exercise Clause. In 1923 the Court held that the protections of the Fourteenth included at least a person's freedom "to worship God according to the dictates of his own conscience . . . ."[18] *Meyer* v. *Nebraska,* 262 U. S. 390, 399. See also *Hamilton* v. *Regents, supra,* at 262. *Cantwell* v. *Connecticut,* 310 U. S. 296, completed in 1940 the process of absorption

[17] See *Barron* v. *Baltimore,* 7 Pet. 243; *Permoli* v. *New Orleans,* 3 How. 589, 609; cf. *Fox* v. *Ohio,* 5 How. 410, 434–435; *Withers* v. *Buckley,* 20 How. 84, 89–91. As early as 1825, however, at least one commentator argued that the guarantees of the Bill of Rights, excepting only those of the First and Seventh Amendments, were meant to limit the powers of the States, Rawle, A View of the Constitution of the United States of America (1825), 120–130.

[18] In addition to the statement of this Court in *Meyer,* at least one state court assumed as early as 1921 that claims of abridgment of the free exercise of religion in the public schools must be tested under the guarantees of the First Amendment as well as those of the state constitution. *Hardwick* v. *Board of School Trustees,* 54 Cal. App. 696, 704–705, 205 P. 49, 52. See Louisell and Jackson, Religion, Theology, and Public Higher Education, 50 Cal. L. Rev. 751, 772 (1962). Even before the Fourteenth Amendment, New York State enacted a general common school law in 1844 which provided that no religious instruction should be given which could be construed to violate the rights of conscience "as secured by the constitution of this state and the United States." N. Y. Laws, 1944, c. 320, § 12.

of the Free Exercise Clause and recognized its dual aspect: the Court affirmed freedom of belief as an absolute liberty, but recognized that conduct, while it may also be comprehended by the Free Exercise Clause, "remains subject to regulation for the protection of society." 310 U. S., at 303–304. This was a distinction already drawn by *Reynolds* v. *United States, supra.* From the beginning this Court has recognized that while government may regulate the behavioral manifestations of religious beliefs, it may not interfere at all with the beliefs themselves.

The absorption of the Establishment Clause has, however, come later and by a route less easily charted. It has been suggested, with some support in history, that absorption of the First Amendment's ban against congressional legislation "respecting an establishment of religion" is conceptually impossible because the Framers meant the Establishment Clause also to foreclose any attempt by Congress to disestablish the existing official state churches.[19] Whether or not such was the understanding of the Framers, and whether such a purpose would have inhibited the absorption of the Establishment Clause at the threshold of the Nineteenth Century are questions not dispositive of our present inquiry. For it is

---

[19] See, *e. g.*, Snee, Religious Disestablishment and the Fourteenth Amendment, 1954 Wash. U. L. Q. 371, 373–394; Kruse, The Historical Meaning and Judicial Construction of the Establishment of Religion Clause of the First Amendment, 2 Washburn L. J. 65, 84–85, 127–130 (1962); Katz, Religion and American Constitutions, Address at Northwestern University Law School, March 20, 1963, pp. 6–7. But see the debate in the Constitutional Convention over the question whether it was necessary or advisable to include among the enumerated powers of the Congress a power "to establish an University, in which no preferences or distinctions should be allowed on account of religion." At least one delegate thought such an explicit delegation "is not necessary," for "[t]he exclusive power at the Seat of Government, will reach the object." The proposal was defeated by only two votes. 2 Farrand, Records of the Federal Convention of 1787 (1911), 616.

clear on the record of history that the last of the formal
state establishments was dissolved more than three dec-
ades before the Fourteenth Amendment was ratified, and
thus the problem of protecting official state churches from
federal encroachments could hardly have been any concern of those who framed the post-Civil War Amendments.[20]   Any such objective of the First Amendment,
having become historical anachronism by 1868, cannot be
thought to have deterred the absorption of the Establishment Clause to any greater degree than it would, for
example, have deterred the absorption of the Free Exercise Clause.   That no organ of the Federal Government
possessed in 1791 any power to restrain the interference
of the States in religious matters is indisputable.   See
Permoli v. *New Orleans,* 3 How. 589.   It is equally plain,
on the other hand, that the Fourteenth Amendment
created a panoply of new federal rights for the protection of citizens of the various States.   And among
those rights was freedom from such state governmental
involvement in the affairs of religion as the Establishment
Clause had originally foreclosed on the part of Congress.

It has also been suggested that the "liberty" guaranteed
by the Fourteenth Amendment logically cannot absorb
the Eastablishment Clause because that clause is not one
of the provisions of the Bill of Rights which in terms protects a "freedom" of the individual.   See Corwin, A Constitution of Powers in a Secular State (1951), 113–116.
The fallacy in this contention, I think, is that it under-

---

[20] The last formal establishment, that of Massachusetts, was dissolved in 1833.   The process of disestablishment in that and other
States is described in Cobb, The Rise of Religious Liberty in America
(1902), c. X; Sweet, The Story of Religion in America (1950), c.
XIII.   The greater relevance of conditions existing at the time of
adoption of the Fourteenth Amendment is suggested in Note, State
Sunday Laws and the Religious Guarantees of the Federal Constitution, 73 Harv. L. Rev. 729, 739, n. 79 (1960).

estimates the role of the Establishment Clause as a co-guarantor, with the Free Exercise Clause, of religious liberty. The Framers did not entrust the liberty of religious beliefs to either clause alone. The Free Exercise Clause "was not to be the full extent of the Amendment's guarantee of freedom from governmental intrusion in matters of faith." *McGowan* v. *Maryland, supra,* at 464 (opinion of Frankfurter, J.).

Finally, it has been contended that absorption of the Establishment Clause is precluded by the absence of any intention on the part of the Framers of the Fourteenth Amendment to circumscribe the residual powers of the States to aid religious activities and institutions in ways which fell short of formal establishments.[21] That argument relies in part upon the express terms of the abortive Blaine Amendment—proposed several years after the adoption of the Fourteenth Amendment—which would have added to the First Amendment a provision that "[n]o state shall make any law respecting an establishment of religion . . . ." Such a restriction would have been superiluous, it is said, if the Fourteenth Amend-

---

[21] See Corwin, A Constitution of Power in a Secular State (1951), 111–114; Fairman and Morrison, Does the Fourteenth Amendment Incorporate the Bill of Rights?, 2 Stan. L. Rev. 5 (1949); Meyer, Comment, The Blaine Amendment and the Bill of Rights, 64 Harv. L. Rev. 939 (1951); Howe, Religion and Race in Public Education, 8 Buffalo L. Rev. 242, 245–247 (1959). Cf. Cooley, Principles of Constitutional Law (2d ed. 1891), 213–214. Compare Professor Freund's comment:

"Looking back, it is hard to see how the Court could have done otherwise, how it could have persisted in accepting freedom of contract as a guaranteed liberty without giving equal status to freedom of press and speech, assembly, and religious observance. What does not seem so inevitable is the inclusion within the Fourteenth Amendment of the concept of nonestablishment of religion in the sense of forbidding nondiscriminatory aid to religion, where there is no interference with freedom of religious exercise." Freund, The Supreme Court of the United States (1961), 58–59.

ment had already made the Establishment Clause binding upon the States.

The argument proves too much, for the Fourteenth Amendment's protection of the free exercise of religion can hardly be questioned; yet the Blaine Amendment would also have added an explicit protection against state laws abridging that liberty.[22] Even if we assume that the draftsmen of the Fourteenth Amendment saw no immediate connection between its protections against state action infringing personal liberty and the guarantees of the First Amendment, it is certainly too late in the day to suggest that their assumed inattention to the question dilutes the force of these constitutional guarantees in their application to the States.[23] It is enough to conclude

---

[22] The Blaine Amendment, 4 Cong. Rec. 5580, included also a more explicit provision that "no money raised by taxation in any State for the support of public schools or derived from any public fund therefor, nor any public lands devoted thereto, shall ever be under the control of any religious sect or denomination . . . ." The Amendment passed the House but failed to obtain the requisite two-thirds vote in the Senate. See 4 Cong. Rec. 5595. The prohibition which the Blaine Amendment would have engrafted onto the American Constitution has been incorporated in the constitutions of other nations; compare Article 28 (1) of the Constitution of India ("No religious instruction shall be provided in any educational institution wholly maintained out of State funds"); Article XX of the Constitution of Japan (". . . the State and its organs shall refrain from religious education or any other religious activity.") See 1 Chaudhri, Constitutional Rights and Limitations (1955), 875, 876.

[23] Three years after the adoption of the Fourteenth Amendment, Mr. Justice Bradley wrote a letter expressing his views on a proposed constitutional amendment designed to acknowledge the dependence of the Nation upon God, and to recognize the Bible as the foundation of its laws and the supreme ruler of its conduct:

"I have never been able to see the necessity or expediency of the movement for obtaining such an amendment. The Constitution was evidently framed and adopted by the people of the United States with the fixed determination to allow absolute religious freedom and equality, and to avoid all appearance even of a State religion, or a

that the religious liberty embodied in the Fourteenth Amendment would not be viable if the Constitution were interpreted to forbid only establishments ordained by Congress.[24]

State endorsement of any particular creed or religious sect. . . . And after the Constitution in its original form was adopted, the people made haste to secure an amendment that Congress shall make no law respecting an establishment of religion, or prohibiting the free exercise thereof. This shows the earnest desire of our Revolutionary fathers that religion should be left to the free and voluntary action of the people themselves. I do not regard it as manifesting any hostility to religion, but as showing a fixed determination to leave the people entirely free on the subject.

"And it seems to me that our fathers were wise; that the great voluntary system of this country is quite as favorable to the promotion of real religion as the systems of governmental protection and patronage have been in other countries. And whilst I do not understand that the association which you represent desire to invoke any governmental interference, still the amendment sought is a step in that direction which our fathers (quite as good Christians as ourselves) thought it wise not to take. In this country they thought they had settled one thing at least, that it is not the province of government to teach theology.

". . . Religion, as the basis and support of civil government, must reside, not in the written Constitution, but in the people themselves. And we cannot legislate religion into the people. It must be infused by gentler and wiser methods." Miscellaneous Writings of Joseph P. Bradley (1901), 357–359.

For a later phase of the controversy over such a constitutional amendment as that which Justice Bradley opposed, see Finlator, Christ in Congress, 4 J. Church and State 205 (1962).

[24] There is no doubt that, whatever "establishment" may have meant to the Framers of the First Amendment in 1791, the draftsmen of the Fourteenth Amendment three quarters of a century later understood the Establishment Clause to foreclose many incidental forms of governmental aid to religion which fell far short of the creation or support of an official church. The Report of a Senate Committee as early as 1853, for example, contained this view of the Establishment Clause:

"If Congress has passed, or should pass, any law which, fairly construed, has in any degree introduced, or should attempt to intro-

The issue of what particular activities the Establishment Clause forbids the States to undertake is our more immediate concern. In *Everson* v. *Board of Education,* 330 U. S. 1, 15–16, a careful study of the relevant history led the Court to the view, consistently recognized in decisions since *Everson,* that the Establishment Clause embodied the Framers' conclusion that government and religion have discrete interests which are mutually best served when each avoids too close a proximity to the other. It is not only the nonbeliever who fears the injection of sectarian doctrines and controversies into the civil polity, but in as high degree it is the devout believer who fears the secularization of a creed which becomes too deeply involved with and dependent upon the government.[25]   It

----

duce, in favor of any church, or ecclestiastical association, or system of religious faith, all or any one of these obnoxious particulars—endowment at the public expense, peculiar privileges to its members, or disadvantages or penalties upon those who should reject its doctrines or belong to other communions—such law would be a 'law respecting an establishment of religion,' and, therefore, in violation of the Constitution."   S. Rep. No. 376, 32d Cong., 2d Sess. 1–2.

Compare Thomas M. Cooley's exposition in the year in which the Fourteenth Amendment was ratified:

"Those things which are not lawful under any of the American constitutions may be stated thus:—

"1. Any law respecting an establishment of religion. . . .

"2. Compulsory support, by taxation or otherwise, of religious instruction.   Not only is no one denomination to be favored at the expense of the rest, but all support of religious instruction must be entirely voluntary."   Cooley, Constitutional Limitations (1st ed. 1868), 469.

[25] Compare, *e. g.,* Miller, Roger Williams: His Contribution to the American Tradition (1953), 83; with Madison, Memorial and Remonstrance Against Religious Assessments, reprinted as an Appendix to the dissenting opinion of Mr. Justice Rutledge, *Everson* v. *Board of Education, supra,* at 63–72.   See also Cahn, On Government and Prayer, 37 N. Y. U. L. Rev. 981, 982–985 (1962); Jefferson's Bill for Establishing Religious Freedom, in Padover, The Complete Jefferson (1943), 946–947; Moulton and Myers, Report

has rightly been said of the history of the Establishment Clause that "our tradition of civil liberty rests not only on the secularism of a Thomas Jefferson but also on the fervent sectarianism . . . of a Roger Williams." Freund, The Supreme Court of the United States (1961), 84.

Our decisions on questions of religious education or exercises in the public schools have consistently reflected this dual aspect of the Establishment Clause. *Engel* v. *Vitale* unmistakably has its roots in three earlier cases which, on cognate issues, shaped the contours of the Establishment Clause. First, in *Everson* the Court held that reimbursement by the town of parents for the cost of transporting their children by public carrier to parochial (as well as public and private nonsectarian) schools did not offend the Establishment Clause. Such reimbursement, by easing the financial burden upon Catholic parents, may indirectly have fostered the operation of the Catholic schools, and may thereby indirectly have facilitated the teaching of Catholic principles, thus serving ultimately a religious goal. But this form of governmental assistance was difficult to distinguish from myriad other incidental if not insignificant government benefits enjoyed by religious institutions—fire and police protection, tax exemptions, and the pavement of streets and sidewalks, for example. "The State contributes no money to the schools. It does not support them. Its legislation, as applied, does no more than provide a general program to help parents get their children, regardless of their religion, safely and expeditiously to and from accredited schools." 330 U. S., at 18. Yet even this form of assistance was thought by four Justices of the *Everson* Court to be barred by the Establishment Clause

on Appointing Chaplains to the Legislature of New York, in Blau, Cornerstones of Religious Freedom in America (1949), 141–156; Bury, A History of Freedom of Thought (2d ed. 1952), 75–76.

because too perilously close to that public support of religion forbidden by the First Amendment.

The other two cases, *Illinois ex rel. McCollum* v. *Board of Education,* 333 U. S. 203, and *Zorach* v. *Clauson,* 343 U. S. 306, can best be considered together. Both involved programs of released time for religious instruction of public school students. I reject the suggestion that *Zorach* overruled *McCollum* in silence.[26] The distinction which the Court drew in *Zorach* between the two cases is in my view faithful to the function of the Establishment Clause.

I should first note, however, that *McCollum* and *Zorach* do not seem to me distinguishable in terms of the free exercise claims advanced in both cases.[27] The nonparticipant in the *McCollum* program was given secular instruction in a separate room during the times his classmates had religious lessons; the nonparticipant in any *Zorach* program also received secular instruction, while his classmates repaired to a place outside the school for religious instruction.

The crucial difference, I think, was that the *McCollum* program offended the Establishment Clause while the *Zorach* program did not. This was not, in my view, because of the difference in public expenditures involved. True, the *McCollum* program involved the regular use of school facilities, classrooms, heat and light and time from the regular school day—even though the actual incremental cost may have been negligible. All religious instruction under the *Zorach* program, by contrast, was

---

[26] See, *e. g.,* Spicer, The Supreme Court and Fundamental Freedoms (1959), 83–84; Kauper, Church, State and Freedom: A Review, 52 Mich. L. Rev. 829, 839 (1954); Reed, Church-State and the Zorach Case, 27 Notre Dame Lawyer 529, 539–541 (1952).

[27] See 343 U. S., at 321–322 (Frankfurter, J., dissenting); Kurland, Religion and the Law (1962), 89. I recognize that there is a question whether in *Zorach* the free exercise claims asserted were in fact proved. 343 U. S., at 311.

carried on entirely off the school premises, and the teacher's part was simply to facilitate the children's release to the churches. The deeper difference was that the *McCullom* program placed the religious instructor in the public school classroom in precisely the position of authority held by the regular teachers of secular subjects, while the *Zorach* program did not.[28] The *McCollum* pro-

---

[28] Mr. Justice Frankfurter described the effects of the *McCollum* program thus:

"Religious education so conducted on school time and property is patently woven into the working scheme of the school. The Champaign arrangement thus presents powerful elements of inherent pressure by the school system in the interest of religious sects. . . . As a result, the public school system of Champaign actively furthers inculcation in the religious tenets of some faiths, and in the process sharpens the consciousness of religious differences at least among some of the children committed to its care." 333 U. S., at 227–228.

For similar reasons some state courts have enjoined the public schools from employing or accepting the services of members of religious orders even in the teaching of secular subjects, *e. g., Zellers* v. *Huff*, 55 N. M. 501, 236 P. 2d 949; *Berghorn* v. *Reorganized School Dist. No. 8*, 364 Mo. 121, 260 S. W. 2d 573; compare ruling of Texas Commissioner of Education, Jan. 25, 1961, in 63 American Jewish Yearbook (1962), 188. Over a half century ago a New York court sustained a school board's exclusion from the public schools of teachers wearing religious garb on similar grounds:

"Then all through the school hours these teachers . . . were before the children as object lessons of the order and church of which they were members. It is within our common observation that young children . . . are very susceptible to the influence of their teachers and of the kind of object lessons continually before them in schools conducted under these circumstances and with these surroundings." *O'Connor* v. *Hendrick*, 109 App. Div. 361, 371–372, 96 N. Y. Supp. 161, 169. See also *Commonwealth* v. *Herr*, 229 Pa. 132, 78 A. 68; Comment, Religious Garb in the Public Schools—A Study in Conflicting Liberties, 22 U. of Chi. L. Rev. 888 (1955).

Also apposite are decisions of several courts which have enjoined the use of parochial schools as part of the public school system, *Harfst* v. *Hoegen*, 349 Mo. 808, 163 S. W. 2d 609; or have invalidated programs for the distribution in public school classrooms of Gideon

gram, in lending to the support of sectarian instruction all the authority of the governmentally operated public school system, brought government and religion into that proximity which the Establishment Clause forbids. To be sure, a religious teacher presumably commands substantial respect and merits attention in his own right. But the Constitution does not permit that prestige and capacity for influence to be augmented by investiture of all the symbols of authority at the command of the lay teacher for the enhancement of secular instruction.

More recent decisions have further etched the contours of Establishment. In the *Sunday Law Cases,* we found in state laws compelling a uniform day of rest from worldly labor no violation of the Establishment Clause (*McGowan* v. *Maryland,* 366 U. S. 420). The basic ground of our decision was that, granted the Sunday Laws

Bibles, *Brown* v. *Orange County Board of Public Instruction,* 128 So. 2d 181 (Fla. App.); *Tudor* v. *Board of Education,* 14 N. J. 31, 100 A. 2d 857. See Note, The First Amendment and Distribution of Religious Literature in the Public Schools, 41 Va. L. Rev. 789, 803–806 (1955). In *Tudor,* the court stressed the role of the public schools in the Bible program:

". . . the public school machinery is used to bring about the distribution of these Bibles to the children . . . . In the eyes of the pupils and their parents the board of education has placed its stamp of approval upon this distribution and, in fact, upon the Gideon Bible itself. . . . This is more than mere 'accommodation' of religion permitted in the Zorach case. The school's part in this distribution is an active one and cannot be sustained on the basis of a mere assistance to religion." 14 N. J., at 51–52, 100 A. 2d, at 868.

The significance of the teacher's authority was recognized by one early state court decision:

"The school being in session, the right to command was vested in the teacher, and the duty of obedience imposed upon the pupils. Under such circumstances a request and a command have the same meaning. A request from one in authority is understood to be a mere euphemism. It is in fact a command in an inoffensive form." *State ex rel. Freeman* v. *Scheve,* 65 Neb. 876, 880, 93 N. W. 169, 170.

were first enacted for religious ends, they were continued in force for reasons wholly secular, namely, to provide a universal day of rest and ensure the health and tranquillity of the community. In other words, government may originally have decreed a Sunday day of rest for the impermissible purpose of supporting religion but abandoned that purpose and retained the laws for the permissible purpose of furthering overwhelmingly secular ends.

Such was the evolution of the contours of the Establishment Clause before *Engel* v. *Vitale.* There, a year ago, we held that the daily recital of the state composed Regents' Prayer constituted an establishment of religion because, although the prayer itself revealed no *sectarian* content or purpose, its nature and meaning were quite clearly *religious.* New York, in authorizing its recitation, had not maintained that distance between the public and the religious sectors commanded by the Establishment Clause when it placed the "power, prestige and financial support of government" behind the prayer. In *Engel,* as in *McCollum,* it did not matter that the amount of time and expense allocated to the daily recitation was small so long as the exercise itself was manifestly religious. Nor did it matter that few children had complained of the practice, for the measure of the seriousness of a breach of the Establishment Clause has never been thought to be the number of people who complain of it.

We also held two Terms ago in *Torcaso* v. *Watkins, supra,* that a State may not constitutionally require an applicant for the office of Notary Public to swear or affirm that he believes in God. The problem of that case was strikingly similar to the issue presented 18 years before in the flag salute case, *West Virginia Board of Education* v. *Barnette, supra.* In neither case was there any claim of establishment of religion, but only of infringement of the individual's religious liberty—in the one case that of the nonbeliever who could not attest to a belief in God; in the other, that of the child whose creed forbade him to salute the flag. But *Torcaso* added a new element not present in *Barnette.* The Maryland test oath involved an attempt to employ essentially religious (albeit non-sectarian) means to achieve a secular goal to which the means bore no reasonable relationship. No one doubted the State's interest in the integrity of its Notaries Public, but that interest did not warrant the screening of applicants by means of a religious test. The *Sunday Law Cases* were different in that respect. Even if Sunday Laws retain certain religious vestiges, they are enforced today for essentially secular objectives which cannot be effectively achieved in modern society except by designating Sunday as the universal day of rest. The Court's opinions cited very substantial problems in selecting or enforcing an alternative day of rest. But the teaching of both *Torcaso* and the *Sunday Law Cases* is that government may not employ religious means to serve secular interests, however legitimate they may be, at least without the clearest demonstration that nonreligious means will not suffice.[29]

---

[29] See for other illustrations of the principle that where First Amendment freedoms are or may be affected, government must employ those means which will least inhibit the exercise of constitutional liberties, *Lovell* v. *Griffin,* 303 U. S. 444; *Schneider* v. *State,* 308 U. S. 147, 161; *Martin* v. *Struthers,* 319 U. S. 141; *Saia* v. *New York,* 334 U. S. 558; *Shelton* v. *Tucker,* 364 U. S. 479, 488–489; *Bantam Books, Inc.,* v. *Sullivan,* 372 U. S. 58, 66, 69–71. See also Note, State Sunday Laws and the Religious Guarantees of the Federal Constitution, 73 Harv. L. Rev. 729, 743–745 (1960); Freund, The Supreme Court of the United States (1961), 86–87; 74 Harv. L. Rev. 613 (1961). And compare *Miller* v. *Cooper,* 56 N. M. 355, 244 P. 2d 520 (1952), in which a state court permitted the holding of public school commencement exercises in a church building only because no public buildings in the community were adequate to accommodate the ceremony.

IV.

I turn now to the cases before us.[30] The religious nature of the exercises here challenged seems plain. Unless *Engel* v. *Vitale* is to be overruled, or we are to engage in wholly disingenuous distinction, we cannot sus-

---

[30] No question has been raised in these cases concerning the standing of these parents to challenge the religious practices conducted in the schools which their children presently attend. Whatever authority *Doremus* v. *Board of Education,* 342 U. S. 429, might have on the question of the standing of one not the parent of children affected by the challenged exercises is not before us in these cases. Neither in *McCollum* nor in *Zorach* was there any reason to question the standing of the parent-plaintiffs under settled principles of justiciability and jurisdiction, whether or not their complaints alleged pecuniary loss or monetary injury. The free-exercise claims of the parents alleged injury sufficient to give them standing. If, however, the gravamen of the lawsuit were exclusively one of establishment, it might seem illogical to confer standing upon a parent who—though he is concededly in the best position to assert a free-exercise claim—suffers no financial injury, by reason of being a parent, different from that of the ordinary taxpayer, whose standing may be open to question. See Sutherland, Establishment According to *Engel,* 76 Harv. L. Rev. 25, 41–43 (1962). I would suggest several answers to this conceptual difficulty. First, the parent is surely the person most directly and immediately concerned about and affected by the challenged establishment, and to deny him standing either in his own right or on behalf of his child might effectively foreclose judicial inquiry into serious breaches of the prohibitions of the First Amendment—even though no special monetary injury could be shown. See *Schempp* v. *School District of Abington Township,* 177 F. Supp. 398, 407; Kurland, The Regents' Prayer Case: "Full of Sound and Fury, Signifying . . . ," 1962 Supreme Court Review 1, 22. Second, the complaint in every case thus far challenging an establishment has set forth at least a colorable claim of infringement of free exercise. When the complaint includes both claims, and neither is frivolous, it would surely be over-technical to say that a parent who does not detail the monetary cost of the exercises to him may ask the court to pass only upon the free-exercise claim, however logically the two may be related. Cf. *Pierce* v. *Society of Sisters, supra; Truax* v. *Raich,* 239

tain these practices. Daily recital of the Lord's Prayer and the reading of passages of Scripture are quite as clearly breaches of the command of the Establishment Clause as was the daily use of the rather bland Regents' Prayer in the New York,public schools. Indeed, I would suppose that if anything the Lord's Prayer and the Holy Bible are more clearly sectarian, and the present violations of the First Amendment consequently more serious. But the religious exercises challenged in these cases have a long history. And almost from the beginning, Bible reading and daily prayer in the schools have been the subject of debate, criticism by educators and other public officials, and proscription by courts and legislative councils. At the outset, then, we must carefully canvass both aspects of this history.

The use of prayers and Bible readings at the opening of the school day long antedates the founding of our Republic. The Rules of the New Haven Hopkins Grammar School required in 1684 "[t]hat the Scholars being

---

U. S. 33, 38–39; *NAACP* v. *Alabama ex rel. Patterson,* 357 U. S. 449, 458–460; *Bell* v. *Hood,* 327 U. S. 678; *Bantam Books, Inc.,* v. *Sullivan,* 372 U. S. 58, 64, n. 6. Finally, the concept of standing is a necessarily flexible one, designed principally to ensure that the plaintiffs have "such a personal stake in the outcome of the controversy as to assure that concrete adverseness which sharpens the presentation of issues upon which the court so largely depends for illumination of difficult constitutional questions . . . ." *Baker* v. *Carr,* 369 U. S. 186, 204. It seems to me that even a cursory examination of the complaints in these two cases and the opinions below discloses that these parents have very real grievances against the respective school authorities which cannot be resolved short of constitutional adjudication. See generally Arthur Garfield Hays Civil Liberties Conference: Public Aid to Parochial Schools and Standing to Bring Suit, 12 Buffalo L. Rev. 35 (1962); Jaffe, Standing to Secure Judicial Review: Public Actions, 74 Harv. L. Rev. 1265 (1961); Sutherland, Due Process and Disestablishment, 62 Harv. L. Rev. 1306, 1327–1332 (1949); Comment, The Supreme Court, the First Amendment, and Religion in the Public Schools, 63 Col. L. Rev. 73, 94, n. 153 (1963).

called together, the Mr. shall every morning begin his work with a short prayer for a blessing on his Laboures and their learning . . . ." [31]   More rigorous was the provision in a 1682 contract with a Dutch schoolmaster in Flatbush, New York:

> "When the school begins, one of the children shall read the morning prayer, as it stands in the catechism, and close with the prayer before dinner; in the afternoon it shall begin with the prayer after dinner, and end with the evening prayer. The evening school shall begin with the Lord's prayer, and close by singing a psalm." [32]

After the Revolution, the new States uniformly continued these long established practices in the private and the few public grammar schools.   The school committee of Boston in 1789, for example, required the city's several schoolmasters "daily to commence the duties of their office by prayer and reading a portion of the Sacred Scriptures . . . ." [33]   That requirement was mirrored throughout the original States, and exemplified the universal practice well into the nineteenth century.   As the free public schools gradually supplanted the private academies and sectarian schools between 1800 and 1850, morning devotional exercises were retained with few alterations.   Indeed, public pressures upon school administrators in many parts of the country would hardly have condoned abandonment of practices to which a century or more of private religious education had accustomed the American people.[34]   The controversy centered, in

---

[31] Quoted in Dunn, What Happened to Religion Education? (1958), 21.

[32] Quoted, *id.*, at 22.

[33] Quoted in Hartford, Moral Values in Public Education: Lessons From the Kentucky Experience (1958), 31.

[34] See Culver, Horace Mann and Religion in the Massachusetts Public Schools (1929), for an account of one prominent educator's

fact, principally about the elimination of plainly sectarian practices and textbooks, and led to the eventual
substitution of nonsectarian, though still religious, exercises and materials.[35]

Statutory provision for daily religious exercises is,
however, of quite recent origin.   At the turn of this century, there was but one State—Massachusetts—which
had a law making morning prayer or Bible reading obligatory.   Statutes elsewhere either permitted such practices
or simply left the question to local option.   It was not
until after 1910 that 11 more States, within a few years,
joined Massachusetts in making one or both exercises
compulsory.[36]   The Pennsylvania law with which we are

---

efforts to satisfy both the protests of those who opposed continuation
of sectarian lessons and exercises in public schools, and the demands
of those who insisted upon the retention of some essentially religious
practices.   Mann's continued use of the Bible for what he regarded
as nonsectarian exercises represented his response to these cross-
pressures.   See Mann, Religious Education, in Blau, Cornerstones
of Religious Freedom in America (1949), 163–201 (from the Twelfth
Annual Report for 1848 of the Secretary of the Board of Education
of Massachusetts).   See also Boles, The Bible, Religion, and the
Public Schools (1961), 22–27.

[35] See 2 Stokes, Church and State in the United States (1950),
572–579; Greene, Religion and the State: The Making and Testing
of an American Tradition (1941), 122–126.

[36] E. g., Ala. Code, Tit. 52, § 542; Del. Code Ann., Tit. 14, §§ 4101–
4102; Fla. Stat. Ann. § 231.09 (2); Mass. Ann. Laws, c. 71, § 31;
Tenn. Code Ann. § 49–1307 (4).   Some statutes, like the recently
amended Pennsylvania statute involved in Schempp, provide for
the excusal or exemption of children whose parents do not wish them
to participate.   See generally Johnson and Yost, Separation of
Church and State in the United States (1948), 33–36; Thayer, The
Role of the School in American Society (1960), 374–375; Beth, The
American Theory of Church and State (1958), 106–107.   Compare
with the American statutory approach Article 28 (3) of the Constitution of India:

"(3) No person attending any educational institution recognised
by the State or receiving aid out of State funds shall be required to

concerned in the *Schempp* case, for example, took effect in 1913; and even the Rule of the Baltimore School Board involved in the *Murray* case dates only from 1905. In no State has there ever been a constitutional or statutory prohibition against the recital of prayers or the reading of scripture, although a number of States have outlawed these practices by judicial decision or administrative order. What is noteworthy about the panoply of state and local regulations from which these cases emerge is the relative recency of the statutory codification of practices which have ancient roots, and the rather small number of States which have ever prescribed compulsory religious exercises in the public schools.

The purposes underlying the adoption and perpetuation of these practices are somewhat complex. It is beyond question that the religious benefits and values realized from daily prayer and Bible reading have usually been considered paramount, and sufficient to justify the continuation of such practices. To Horace Mann, embroiled in an intense controversy over the role of *sectarian* instruction and textbooks in the Boston public schools, there was little question that the regular use of the Bible—which he thought essentially nonsectarian—would bear fruit in the spiritual enlightenment of his pupils.[37] A contemporary of Mann's, the Commissioner of Education of a neighboring State, expressed a view which many enlightened educators of that day shared:

"As a textbook of morals the Bible is pre-eminent, and should have a prominent place in our schools,

---

take part in any religious instruction that may be imparted in such institution or to attend any religious worship that may be conducted in such institution or in any premises attached thereto unless such person or, if such person is a minor, his guardian has given his consent thereto." See 1 Chaudhri, Constitutional Rights and Limitations (1955), 876, 939.

[37] See note 34, *supra.*

> either as a reading book or as a source of appeal and instruction. Sectarianism, indeed, should not be countenanced in the schools; but the Bible is not sectarian . . . . The Scriptures should at least be read at the opening of the school, if no more. Prayer may also be offered with the happiest effects.".[38]

Wisconsin's Superintendent of Public Instruction, writing a few years later in 1858, reflected the attitude of his eastern colleagues, in that he regarded "with special favor the use of the Bible in public schools, as pre-eminently first in importance among text-books for teaching the noblest principles of virtue, morality, patriotism and good order—love and reverence for God—charity and good will to man." [39]

Such statements reveal the understanding of educators that the daily religious exercises in the schools served broader goals than compelling formal worship of God or fostering church attendance. The religious aims of the educators who adopted and retained such exercises were comprehensive, and in many cases quite devoid of sectarian bias—but the crucial fact is that they were nonetheless religious. While it has been suggested, see pp. 50–53, *infra,* that daily prayer and reading of scripture now serve secular goals as well, there can be no doubt that the origins of these practices were unambiguously religious, even where the educator's aim was not to win adherents to a particular creed or faith.

Almost from the beginning religious exercises in the public schools have been the subject of intense criticism, vigorous debate, and judicial or administrative prohibition. Significantly, educators and school boards

---

[38] Quoted from New Hampshire School Reports, 1850, 31–32, in Kinney, Church and State: The Struggle for Separation in New Hampshire, 1630–1900 (1955), 157–158.

[39] Quoted in Boyer, Religious Education of Public School Pupils in Wisconsin, 1953 Wis. L. Rev. 181, 185.

early entertained doubts about both the legality and the soundness of opening the school day with compulsory prayer or Bible reading. Particularly in the large Eastern cities, where immigration had exposed the public schools to religious diversities and conflicts unknown to the homogeneous academies of the eighteenth century, local authorities found it necessary even before the Civil War to seek an accommodation. In 1843, the Philadelphia School Board adopted the following resolutions:

> "RESOLVED, that no children be required to attend or unite in the reading of the Bible in the Public Schools, whose parents are conscientiously opposed thereto:
>
> "RESOLVED, that those children whose parents conscientiously prefer and desire any particular version of the Bible, without note or comment, be furnished the same." [40]

A decade later, the Superintendent of Schools of New York State issued an even bolder decree that prayers could no longer be required as part of public school activities, and that where the King James Bible was read, Catholic students could not be compelled to attend.[41] This type of accommodation was not restricted to the East Coast; the Cincinnati Board of Education resolved in 1869 that "religious instruction and the reading of religious books, including the Holy Bible, are prohibited in the common schools of Cincinnati, it being the true object and intent of this rule to allow the children of the parents of all sects and opinions, in matters of faith and worship,

---

[40] Quoted in Dunn, What Happened to Religious Education? (1958), 271.

[41] Quoted in Butts, The American Tradition in Religion and Education (1950), 135–136.

to enjoy alike the benefit of the common-school fund." [42]
The Board repealed at the same time an earlier regulation
which had required the singing of hymns and psalms to
accompany the Bible reading at the start of the school
day. And in 1889, one commentator ventured the view
that "[t]here is not enough to be gained from Bible reading to justify the quarrel that has been raised over it." [43]

Thus a great deal of controversy over religion in the
public schools had preceded the debate over the Blaine
Amendment, precipitated by President Grant's insistence
that matters of religion should be left "to the family altar,
the church, and the private school, supported entirely by
private contributions." [44] There was ample precedent,
too, for Theodore Roosevelt's declaration that in the
interest of "absolutely nonsectarian public schools" it
was "not our business to have the Protestant Bible or the
Catholic Vulgate or the Talmud read in those schools." [45]
The same principle appeared in the message of an Ohio
Governor who vetoed a compulsory Bible-reading bill in
1925:

> "It is my belief that religious teaching in our
> homes, Sunday schools, churches, by the good

[42] See *Board of Education* v. *Minor,* 23 Ohio St. 211; Blakely,
American State Papers and Related Documents on Freedom in Religion (4th rev. ed. 1949), 864.

[43] Report of the United States Commissioner of Education for the
Year 1888–1889, part I, H. R. Exec. Doc. No. 1, part 5, 51st Cong., 1st
Sess. 627.

[44] Quoted in *Illinois ex rel. McCollum* v. *Board of Education,
supra,* at 218 (opinion of Frankfurter, J.). See also President
Grant's Annual Message to Congress, Dec. 7, 1875, 4 Cong. Rec. 175
et seq., which apparently inspired the drafting and submission of
the Blaine Amendment. See Meyer, Comment, The Blaine Amendment and the Bill of Rights, 64 Harv. L. Rev. 939 (1951).

[45] Theodore Roosevelt to Michael A. Schaap, Feb. 22, 1915, 8
Letters of Theodore Roosevelt (Morison ed. 1954), 893.

> mothers, fathers and ministers of Ohio is far prefer-
> able to compulsory teaching of religion by the state.
> The spirit of our federal and state constitutions from
> the beginning . . . [has] been to leave religious
> instruction to the discretion of parents." [46]

The same theme has recurred in the opinions of the
Attorneys General of several States holding religious exercises or instruction to be in violation of the state or federal
constitutional command of separation of church and
state.[47] Thus the basic principle upon which our decision last year in *Engel* v. *Vitale* necessarily rested, and
which we reaffirm today, can hardly be thought to be
radical or novel.

Particularly relevant for our purposes are the decisions
of the state courts on questions of religion in the public
schools. Those decisions, while not, of course, authoritative in this Court, serve nevertheless to define the problem before us and to guide our inquiry. With the growth
of religious diversity and the rise of vigorous dissent it
was inevitable that the courts would be called upon to
enjoin religious practices in the public schools which
offended certain sects and groups. The earliest of such
decisions declined to review the propriety of actions taken
by school authorities, so long as those actions were within

---

[46] Quoted in Boles, The Bible, Religion, and the Public Schools
(1961), 238.

[47] *E. g.*, 26 Ore. Op. Atty. Gen. 46 (1952); 25 Cal. Op. Atty. Gen.
316 (1955); 1948–1950 Nev. Atty. Gen. Rep. 69 (1948). For a 1961
opinion of the Attorney General of Michigan to the same effect, see
63 American Jewish Yearbook (1962) 189. In addition to the Governor of Ohio, see note 46, *supra*, a Governor of Arizona vetoed a
proposed law which would have permitted "reading the Bible, without
comment, except to teach Historical or Literary facts." See 2 Stokes,
Church and State in the United States (1950), 568.

the purview of the administrators' powers.[48] Thus, where the local school board *required* religious exercises, the courts would not enjoin them;[49] and where, as in at least one case, the school officials *forbade* devotional practices, the court refused on similar grounds to overrule that decision.[50] Thus, whichever way the early cases came up, the governing principle of nearly complete deference to administrative discretion effectively foreclosed any consideration of constitutional questions.

The last quarter of the nineteenth century found the courts beginning to question the constitutionality of public school religious exercises. The legal context was still, of course, that of the state constitutions, since the First Amendment had not yet been held applicable to state action. And the state constitutional prohibitions against church-state cooperation or governmental aid to religion were generally less rigorous than the Establishment Clause of the First Amendment. It is therefore remarkable that the courts of a half dozen States found compulsory religious exercises in the public schools in violation of their respective state constitutions.[51] These

---

[48] See Johnson and Yost, Separation of Church and State in the United States (1948), 71; Note, Bible Reading in Public Schools, 9 Vand. L. Rev. 849, 851 (1956).

[49] *E. g., Spiller* v. *Inhabitants of Woburn,* 12 Allen (Mass.) 127 (1866); *Donahoe* v. *Richards,* 38 Maine 376, 413 (1854); cf. *Ferriter* v. *Tyler,* 48 Vt. 444, 471–472 (1876).

[50] *Board of Education* v. *Minor,* 23 Ohio St. 211 (1873).

[51] *People ex rel. Ring* v. *Board of Education,* 245 Ill. 334, 92 N. E. 251 (1910); *Herold* v. *Parish Board of School Directors,* 136 La. 1034, 68 So. 116 (1915); *State ex rel. Weiss* v. *District Board,* 76 Wis. 177, 44 N. W. 967 (1890); *State ex rel. Finger* v. *Weedman,* 55 S. D. 343, 226 N. W. 348 (1929); *State ex rel. Dearle* v. *Frazier,* 102 Wash. 369, 173 P. 35 (1918); cf. *State ex rel. Clithero* v. *Showalter,* 159 Wash. 519, 293 P. 1000 (1930); *State ex rel. Freeman* v. *Scheve,*

courts attributed much significance to the clearly religious origins and content of the challenged practices, and to the impossibility of avoiding sectarian controversy in their conduct. The Illinois Supreme Court expressed in 1910 the principles which characterized these decisions:

> "The public school is supported by taxes which each citizen, regardless of his religion or lack of it, is compelled to pay. The school, like the government, is simply a civil institution. It is secular, and not religious, in its purpose. The truths of the Bible are the truths of religion, which do not come within the province of the public school. . . . No one denies that they should be taught to the youth of the state. The Constitution and the law do not interfere with such teaching, but they do banish theological polemics from the school and the school districts. This is done, not from any hostility to religion, but simply because it is no part of the duty of the state to teach religion—to take the money of all, and apply it to teaching the children of all the religion of a part only. Instruction in religion must be voluntary " *People ex rel. Ring* v. *Board of Education,* 245 I 334, 349, 92 N. E. 251, 256 (1910).

The Supreme Court of South Dakota, in banning devotional exercises from the public schools of that State, also cautioned that "[t]he state as an educator must keep out of this field, and especially is this true in the common schools, where the child is immature, without fixed religious convictions . . . ." *State ex rel. Finger* v. *Weedman,* 55 S. D. 343, 357, 226 N. W. 348, 354 (1929).

---

65 Neb. 853, 91 N. W. 846 (1902), modified, 65 Neb. 876, 93 N. W. 169 (1903). The cases are discussed in Boles, The Bible, Religion, and the Public Schools (1961), c. IV; Harrison, The Bible, the Constitution and Public Education, 29 Tenn. L. Rev. 363, 386–389 (1962).

Even those state courts which have sustained devotional exercises under state law [52] have usually recognized the primarily religious character of prayers and Bible readings. If such practices were not for that reason unconstitutional, it was necessarily because the state constitution forbade only public expenditures for *sectarian* instruction, or for activities which made the schoolhouse a "place of worship," but said nothing about the subtler question of laws "respecting an establishment of religion." [53] Thus the panorama of history permits no

---

[52] *Moore* v. *Monroe,* 64 Iowa 367, 20 N. W. 475 (1884); *Hackett* v. *Brooksville Graded School District,* 120 Ky. 608, 87 S. W. 792 (1905); *Billard* v. *Board of Education,* 69 Kan. 53, 76 P. 422 (1904); *Pfeiffer* v. *Board of Education,* 118 Mich. 560, 77 N. W. 250 (1898); *Kaplan* v. *School District,* 171 Minn. 142, 214 N. W. 18 (1927); *Lewis* v. *Board of Education,* 157 Misc. 520, 285 N. Y. Supp. 164 (Sup. Ct. 1935), modified on other grounds, 247 App. Div. 106, 286 N. Y. Supp. 174 (1936), appeal dismissed, 276 N. Y. 490, 12 N. E. 2d 172 (1937); *Doremus* v. *Board of Education,* 5 N. J. 435, 75 A. 2d 880 (1950), appeal dismissed, 342 U. S. 429; *Church* v. *Bullock,* 104 Tex. 1, 109 S. W. 115 (1908); *People ex rel. Vollmar* v. *Stanley,* 81 Colo. 276, 255 P. 610 (1927); *Wilkerson* v. *City of Rome,* 152 Ga. 762, 110 S. E. 895 (1922); *Carden* v. *Bland,* 199 Tenn. 665, 288 S. W. 2d 718 (1956); *Chamberlin* v. *Dade County Board of Public Instruction,* 143 So. 2d 21 (Fla. 1962).

[53] For discussion of the constitutional and statutory provisions involved in the state cases which sustained devotional exercises in the public schools, see Boles, The Bible, Religion, and the Public Schools (1961), c. III; Harrison, The Bible, the Constitution and Public Education, 29 Tenn. L. Rev. 363, 381–385 (1962); Fellman, Separation of Church and State in the United States: A Summary View, 1950 Wis. L. Rev. 427, 450–452; Note, Bible Reading in Public Schools, 9 Vand. L. Rev. 849, 854–859 (1956); Note, Nineteenth Century Judicial Thought Concerning Church-State Relations, 40 Minn. L. Rev. 672, 675–678 (1956). State courts appear to have been increasingly influenced in sustaining devotional practices by the availability of an excuse or exemption for dissenting students. See Cushman, The Holy Bible and the Public Schools, 40 Cornell L. Q. 475, 477 (1955); 13 Vand. L. Rev. 552 (1960).

other conclusion than that daily prayers and Bible readings in the public schools have always been designed to be, and have been regarded as, essentially religious exercises.   Unlike the Sunday closing laws, these exercises appear neither to have been divorced from their religious origins nor deprived of their centrally religious character by the passage of time,[54] cf. *McGowan* v. *Maryland, supra,* at 442–445.   On this distinction alone we might well rest a constitutional decision.   But three further contentions have been pressed in the argument of these cases.   These contentions deserve careful consideration, for if the position of the school authorities were correct in respect to any of them, we would be misapplying the principles of *Engel* v. *Vitale.*

A.

First, it is argued that however clearly religious may have been the origins and early nature of daily prayer and Bible reading, these practices today serve so clearly secular educational purposes that their religious attributes may be overlooked.   I do not doubt, for example, that morning devotional exercises may foster better discipline in the classroom, and elevate the spiritual level on which the school day opens.   The Pennsylvania Superintendent of Public Instruction, testifying by deposition in the *Schempp* case, offered his view that daily Bible reading "places upon the children or those hearing the reading of this, and the atmosphere which goes on in the reading . . . one of the last vestiges of moral value

---

[54] See Rosenfield, Separation of Church and State in the Public Schools, 22 U. of Pitt. L. Rev. 561, 571–572 (1961); Harrison, The Bible, the Constitution and Public Education, 29 Tenn. L. Rev. 363, 399–400 (1962); 30 Ford. L. Rev. 801, 803 (1962); 45 Va. L. Rev. 1381 (1959).   The essentially religious character of the materials used in these exercises is, in fact, strongly suggested by the presence of excusal or exemption provisions, and by the practice of rotating or alternating the use of different prayers and versions of the Holy Bible.

that we have left in our school system." The exercise thus affords, the Superintendent concluded, "a strong contradiction to the materialistic trends of our time." Baltimore's Superintendent of Schools expressed a similar view of the practices challenged in the *Murray* case, to the effect that "[t]he acknowledgment of the existence of God as symbolized in the opening exercises establishes a discipline tone which tends to cause each individual pupil to constrain his overt acts and to consequently conform to accepted standards of behavior during his attendance at school." These views are by no means novel, see, e. g., *Billard* v. *Board of Education,* 69 Kan. 53, 57–58, 76 P. 422, 423 (1904).[55]

It is not the business of this Court to gainsay the judgments of experts on matters of pedagogy. Such decisions must be left to the discretion of those administrators charged with the supervision of the Nation's public schools. The limited province of the courts is to determine whether the means which the educators have chosen to achieve legitimate pedagogical ends infringe the constitutional freedoms of the First Amendment. The secular purposes which devotional exercises are said to serve fall into two categories—those which depend upon an immediately religious experience shared by the participating children; and those which appear sufficiently divorced from the religious content of the devotional material that they can be served equally by nonreligious

---

[55] In the *Billard* case, the teacher whose use of the Lord's Prayer and the Twenty-third Psalm was before the court, testified that the exercise served disciplinary rather than spiritual purposes:

"It is necessary to have some general exercise after the children come in from the playground to prepare them for their work. You need some exercise to quiet them down."

When asked again if the purpose were not at least partially religious, the teacher replied, "[i]t was religious to the children that are religious, and to the others it was not." 69 Kan., at 57–58, 76 P., at 423.

materials. With respect to the first objective, much has
been written about the moral and spiritual values of
infusing some religious influence or instruction into the
public school classroom.[56] To the extent that only *religious* materials will serve this purpose, it seems to me
that the purpose as well as the means is so plainly religious
that the exercise is necessarily forbidden by the Establishment Clause. The fact that purely secular benefits
may eventually result does not seem to me to justify the
exercises, for similar indirect nonreligious benefits could
no doubt have been claimed for the released time program
invalidated in *McCollum.*

The second justification assumes that religious exercises at the start of the school day may directly serve
solely secular ends—for example, by fostering harmony
and tolerance among the pupils, enhancing the authority
of the teacher, and inspiring better discipline. To the
extent that such benefits result not from the content of
the readings and recitation, but simply from the holding
of such a solemn exercise at the opening assembly or
the first class of the day, it would seem that less sensitive materials might equally well serve the same purpose.

---

[56] See, *e. g.*, Henry, The Place of Religion in Public Schools
(1950); Martin, Our Public Schools—Christian or Secular (1952);
Educational Policies Comm'n of the National Educational Assn.,
Moral and Spiritual Values in the Public Schools (1951), c. IV; Har-
ner, Religion's Place in General Education (1949). Educators are
by no means unanimous, however, on this question. See Boles, The
Bible, Religion, and the Public Schools (1961), 223–224. Compare
George Washington's advice in his Farewell Address:

"And let us with caution indulge the supposition, that morality can
be maintained without religion. Whatever may be conceded to the
influence of refined education on minds of peculiar structure, reason
and experience both forbid us to expect that National moralty can
prevail in exclusion of religious principle." 35 Writings of George
Washington (Fitzpatrick ed. 1940), 229.

I have previously suggested that *Torcaso* and the *Sunday Law Cases* forbid the use of religious means to achieve secular ends where nonreligious means will suffice. That principle is readily applied to these cases. It has not been shown that readings from the speeches and messages of great Americans, for example, or from the documents of our heritage of liberty, daily recitation of the Pledge of Allegiance, or even the observance of a moment of reverent silence at the opening of class, may not adequately serve the solely secular purposes of the devotional activities without jeopardizing either the religious liberties of any members of the community or the proper degree of separation between the spheres of religion and government.[57] Such substitutes would, I think, be unsatisfactory or inadequate only to the extent that the present activities do in fact serve religious goals. While I do not question the judgment of experienced educators that the challenged practices may well achieve valuable secular ends, it seems to me that the State acts unconstitutionally if it either sets about to attain even indirectly religious ends by religious means, or if it uses religious means to serve secular ends where secular means would suffice.

---

[57] Thomas Jefferson's insistence that where the judgments of young children "are not sufficiently matured for religious inquiries, their memories may here be stored with the most useful facts from Grecian, Roman, European and American history," 2 Writings of Thomas Jefferson (Memorial ed. 1903), 204, is relevant here. Recent proposals have explored the possibility of commencing the school day "with a quiet moment that would still the tumult of the playground and start a day of study," Editorial, Washington Post, June 28, 1962, § A, p. 22, col. 2. See also New York Times, Aug. 30, 1962, § 1, p. 18, col. 2. For a consideration of these and other alternative proposals see Choper, Religion in the Public Schools: A Proposed Constitutional Standard, 47 Minn. L. Rev. 329, 370–371 (1963). See also 2 Stokes, Church and State in the United States (1950), 571.

B.

Second, it is argued that the particular practices involved in the two cases before us are unobjectionable because they prefer no particular sect or sects at the expense of others. Both the Baltimore and Abington procedures permit, for example, the reading of any of several versions of the Bible, and this flexibility is said to ensure neutrality sufficiently to avoid the constitutional prohibition. One answer, which might be dispositive, is that any version of the Bible is inherently sectarian, else there would be no need to offer a system of rotation or alternation of versions in the first place, that is, to allow different sectarian versions to be used on different days. The sectarian character of the Holy Bible has been at the core of the whole controversy over religious practices in the public schools throughout its long and often bitter history.[58] To

---

[58] The history, as it bears particularly upon the role of sectarian differences concerning Biblical texts and interpretation, has been summarized in *Tudor* v. *Board of Education,* 14 N. J. 31, 36–44, 100 A. 2d 857, 859–864. See also *State ex rel. Weiss* v. *District Board,* 76 Wis. 177, 190–193, 44 N. W. 967, 972–975. One state court adverted to these differences a half century ago:

"The Bible, in its entirety, is a sectarian book as to the Jew and every believer in any religion other than the Christian religion, and as to those who are heretical or who hold beliefs that are not regarded as orthodox . . . its use in the schools necessarily results in sectarian instruction. There are many sects of Christians, and their differences grow out of their differing constructions of various parts of the Scriptures—the different conclusions drawn as to the effect of the same words. The portions of Scripture which form the basis of these sectarian differences cannot be thoughtfully and intelligently read without impressing the reader, favorably or otherwise, with reference to the doctrines supposed to be derived from them." *People ex rel. Ring* v. *Board of Education,* 245 Ill. 334, 347–348, 92 N. E. 251, 255. But see, for a sharply critical comment, Schofield, Religious Lib-

vary the version as the Abington and Baltimore schools have done may well be less offensive than to read from the King James version every day, as once was the practice. But the result even of this relatively benign procedure is that majority sects are preferred in approximate proportion to their representation in the community and in the student body, while the smaller sects suffer commensurate discrimination. So long as the subject matter of the exercise is sectarian in character, these consequences cannot be avoided.

The argument contains, however, a more basic flaw. There are persons in every community—often deeply devout—to whom any version of the Judaeo-Christian Bible is offensive.[59] There are others whose reverence for

---

erty and Bible Reading in Illinois Public Schools, 6 Ill. L. Rev. 17 (1911).

See also Dunn, What Happened to Religious Education? (1958), 268–273; Dawson, America's Way in Church, State, and Society (1953), 53–54; Johnson and Yost, Separation of Church and State in the United States (1948), c. IV; Harpster, Religion, Education and the Law, 36 Marquette L. Rev. 24, 44–45 (1952); 20 Ohio State L. J. 701, 702–703 (1959).

[59] See *Torcaso* v. *Watkins, supra,* at 495, n. 11; Cushman, The Holy Bible and the Public Schools, 40 Cornell L. Q. 475, 480–483 (1955); Note, Separation of Church and State: Religious Exercises in the Schools, 31 U. of Cinc. L. Rev. 408, 411–412 (1962). Few religious persons today would share the universality of the Biblical canons of John Quincy Adams:

"You ask me *what* Bible I take as the standard of my faith—the Hebrew, the Samaritan, the old English translation, or what? I answer, the Bible containing the sermon upon the mount—any Bible that I can read and understand. . . . I take any one of them for my standard of faith. If Socinus or Priestley had made a fair *translation* of the Bible, I would have taken that, but without their comments." John Quincy Adams to John Adams, Jan. 3, 1817, in Koch and Peden, Selected Writings of John and John Quincy Adams (1946), 292.

the Holy Scriptures demands private study or reflection and to whom public reading or recitation is sacrilegious, as one of the expert witnesses at the trial of the *Schempp* case explained. To such persons it is not the fact of using the Bible in the public schools, nor the content of any particular version, that is offensive, but only the *manner* in which it is used.[60] For such persons, the anathema of public communion is even more pronounced when prayer is involved. Many deeply devout persons have always regarded prayer as a necessarily private experience.[61]

---

[60] Rabbi Solomon Grayzel testified before the District Court, "In Judaism the Bible is not read, it is studied. There is no special virtue attached to a mere reading of the Bible; there is a great deal of virtue attached to a study of the Bible." See Boles, The Bible, Religion, and the Public Schools (1961), 208–218; Choper, Religion in the Public Schools: A Proposed Constitutional Standard, 47 Minn. L. Rev. 329, 372–375 (1963). One religious periodical has suggested the danger that "an observance of this sort is likely to deteriorate quickly into an empty formality with little if any significance. Prescribed forms of this sort, as many colleges have concluded after years of compulsory chapel attendance, can actually work against the inculcation of vital religion." Prayer in the Public School Opposed, 69 Christian Century, Jan. 9, 1952, p. 35.

[61] See Cahn, On Government and Prayer, 37 N. Y. U. L. Rev. 981, 993–994 (1962). A leading Protestant journal recently noted:

"Agitation for removal of religious practices in public schools is not prompted or supported entirely by Jews, humanists, and atheists. At both local and national levels, many Christian leaders, concerned both for civil rights of minorities and for adequate religious education, are opposed to religious exercises in public schools. . . . Many persons, both Jews and Christians, believe that prayer and Bible reading are too sacred to be permitted in public schools in spite of their possible moral value." Smith, The Religious Crisis In Our Schools, 128 The Episcopalian, May 1963, pp. 12–13. See, *e. g.*, for other recent statements on this question, Editorial, Amending the Amendment, 108 America, May 25, 1963, p. 736; Sissel, A Christian View: Behind the Fight Against School Prayer, 27 Look, June 18, 1963, p. 25.

It should be unnecessary to demonstrate that the Lord's Prayer, more clearly than the Regents' Prayer involved in *Engel* v. *Vitale,* is an

One Protestant group recently commented, for example: "When one thinks of prayer as sincere outreach of a human soul to the Creator, 'required prayer' becomes an absurdity." [62] There is a similar problem with respect to comment upon the passages of scripture which are to be read. Most present statutes forbid comment, and this practice accords with the views of many religious groups as to the manner in which the Bible should be read. However, as a recent survey discloses, scriptural passages read without comment frequently convey no message to the younger children in the school. Thus there has developed a practice in some schools of bridging the gap between faith and understanding by means of "definitions," even where "comment" is forbidden by statute. [63]

essentially Christian supplication. See, *e. g.*, Scott, The Lord's Prayer: Its Character, Purpose, and Interpretation (1951), 55; Buttrick, So We Believe, So We Pray (1951), 142; Levy, Lord's Prayer, in 7 Universal Jewish Encyclopedia (1948), 193.

[62] Statement of the Baptist Joint Committee on Public Affairs, in 4 J. Church and State 144 (1962).

[63] See Harrison, The Bible, the Constitution and Public Education, 29 Tenn. L. Rev. 363, 397 (1962). The application of statutes and regulations which forbid comment on scriptural passages is further complicated by the view of certain religious groups that reading without comment is either meaningless or actually offensive. Compare Rabbi Grayzel's testimony before the District Court that "the Bible is misunderstood when it is taken without explanation." A recent survey of the attitudes of certain teachers disclosed concern that "refusal to answer pupil questions regarding any curricular activity is not educationally sound," and that reading without comment might create in the minds of the pupils the impression that something was "hidden or wrong." Boles, The Bible, Religion, and the Public Schools (1961), 235–236. Compare the comment of a foreign observer: "In no other field of learning would we expect a child to draw the full meaning from what he reads without explanatory comment. But comment by the teacher will inevitably reveal his own personal preferences; and the exhibition of preferences is what we are seeking to eliminate." MacKinnon, Freedom?—or Toleration?, The Problem of Church and State in the United States, [1959] Pub. Law 374, 383.

The present practice therefore poses a difficult dilemma: While Bible reading is almost universally required to be without comment, since only by such a prohibition can sectarian interpretation be excluded from the classroom, the rule breaks down at the point at which rudimentary definitions of Biblical terms are necessary for comprehension if the exercise is to be meaningful at all.

It has been suggested that a tentative solution to these problems may lie in the fashioning of a "common core" of theology tolerable to all creeds but preferential to none.[64] But as one commentator has recently observed, "[h]istory is not encouraging to" those who hope to fashion a "common denominator of religion detached from its manifestation in any organized church." Sutherland, Establishment According to *Engel,* 76 Harv. L. Rev. 25, 51 (1962). Thus, the notion of a "common core" litany or supplication offends many deeply devout worshippers who do not find clearly sectarian practices objectionable.[65] Father Gustave Weigel has recently expressed

---

[64] See Abbott, A Common Bible Reader for Public Schools, 56 Religious Education 20 (1961); Note, 22 Albany L. Rev. 156–157 (1958); 2 Stokes, Church and State in the United States (1950), 501–506 (describing the "common denominator" or "three faiths" plan and certain programs of instruction designed to implement the "common core" approach). The attempts to evolve a universal, nondenominational prayer are by no means novel. See, *e. g.*, Madison's letter to Edward Everett, March 19, 1823, commenting upon a "project of a prayer . . . intended to comprehend & conciliate college students of every [Christ]ian denomination, by a Form composed wholly of texts & phrases of scripture." 9 Writings of James Madison (Hunt ed. 1910), 126. For a fuller description of this and other attempts to fashion a "common core" or nonsectarian exercise, see *Engel* v. *Vitale,* 18 Misc. 2d 659, 660–662, 191 N. Y. S. 2d 453, 459–460.

[65] See the policy statement recently drafted by the National Council of the Churches of Christ: ". . . neither true religion nor good education is dependent upon the devotional use of the Bible in the

a widely shared view: "The moral code held by each separate religious community can reductively be unified, but the consistent particular believer wants no such reduction." [66] And, as the American Council on Education warned several years ago, "The notion of a common core suggests a watering down of the several faiths to the point where common essentials appear. This might easily lead to a new sect—a public school sect—which would take its place alongside the existing faiths and compete with them." [67] *Engel* is surely authority that nonsectarian religious practices, equally with sectarian exercises, violate the Establishment Clause. Moreover, even if the Establishment Clause were oblivious to nonsectarian religious practices, I think it quite likely that the "common core" approach would be sufficiently objectionable to many groups to be foreclosed by the prohibitions of the Free Exercise Clause.

----

public school program. . . . Apart from the constitutional questions involved, attempts to establish a 'common core' of religious beliefs to be taught in public schools for the purpose of indoctrination are unrealistic and unwise. Major faith groups have not agreed on a formulation of religious beliefs common to all. Even if they had done so, such a body of religious doctrine would tend to become a substitute for the more demanding commitments of historic faiths." Washington Post, May 25, 1963, § A, p. 1, col. 4. See also Choper, Religion in the Public Schools: A Proposed Constitutional Standard, 47 Minn. L. Rev. 329, 341, 368–369 (1963). See also Hartford, Moral Values in Public Education: Lessons from the Kentucky Experience (1958), 261–262; Moehlman, The Wall of Separation Between Church and State (1951), 158–159. Cf. Mosk, "Establishment Clause" Clarified, 22 Law in Transition 231, 235–236 (1963).

[66] Quoted in Kurland, The Regents' Prayer Case: "Full of Sound and Fury, Signifying . . . .", 1962 Supreme Court Review (1962), 31.

[67] Quoted in Harrison, The Bible, the Constitution and Public Education, 29 Tenn. L. Rev. 363, 417 (1962). See also Dawson, America's Way in Church, State, and Society (1953), 54.

C.

A third element which is said to absolve the practices involved in these cases from the ban of the religious guarantees of the Constitution is the provision to excuse or exempt students who wish not to participate. Insofar as these practices are claimed to violate the Establishment Clause, I find the answer which the District Court gave after our remand of _Schempp_ to be altogether dispositive:

> "The fact that some pupils, or theoretically all pupils, might be excused from attendance at the exercises does not mitigate the obligatory nature of the ceremony . . . . The exercises are held in the school buildings and perforce are conducted by and under the authority of the local school authorities and during school sessions. Since the statute requires the reading of the 'Holy Bible,' a Christian document, the practice, as we said in our first opinion, prefers the Christian religion. The record demonstrates that it was the intention of the General Assembly of the Commonwealth of Pennsylvania to introduce a religious ceremony into the public schools of the Commonwealth." 201 F. Supp., at 819.

Thus the short, and to me sufficient, answer is that the availability of excusal or exemption simply has no relevance to the establishment question, if it is once found that these practices are essentially religious exercises designed at least in part to achieve religious aims through the use of public school facilities during the school day.

The more difficult question, however, is whether the availability of excusal for the dissenting child serves to refute challenges to these practices under the Free Exercise Clause. While it is enough to decide these cases to dispose of the establishment questions, questions of free exercise are so inextricably interwoven into the history and present status of these practices as to justify disposition of this second aspect of the excusal issue. The answer is that the excusal procedure itself necessarily operates in such a way as to infringe the rights of free exercise of those children who wish to be excused. We have held in *Barnette* and *Torcaso,* respectively, that a State may require neither public school students nor candidates for an office of public trust to profess beliefs offensive to religious principles. By the same token the State could not constitutionally require a student to profess publicly his disbelief as the prerequisite to the exercise of his constitutional right of abstention. And apart from *Torcaso* and *Barnette,* I think *Speiser* v. *Randall,* 357 U. S. 513, suggests a further answer. We held there that a State may not condition the grant of a tax exemption upon the willingness of those entitled to the exemption to affirm their loyalty to the Government, even though the exemption was itself a matter of grace rather than of constitutional right. We concluded that to impose upon the eligible taxpayers the affirmative burden of proving their loyalty impermissibly jeopardized the freedom to engage in constitutionally protected activities close to the area to which the loyalty oath related. *Speiser* v. *Randall* seems to me to dispose of two aspects of the excusal or exemption procedure now before us. First, by requiring what is tantamount in the eyes of teachers and schoolmates to a profession of disbelief, or at least of nonconformity, the procedure may well deter those children who do not wish to participate for any reason based upon the dictates of conscience from exercising an indisputably constitutional right to be excused.[68] Thus the excusal

---

[68] See the testimony of Edward L. Schempp, the father of the children in the Abington schools and plaintiffs-appellee in No. 142, concerning his reasons for not asking that his children be excused from

provision in its operation subjects them to a cruel dilemma. In consequence, even devout children may well avoid claiming their right and simply continue to participate in exercises distasteful to them because of an understandable reluctance to be stigmatized as atheists or nonconformists simply on the basis of their request.

Such reluctance to seek exemption seems all the more likely in view of the fact that children are disinclined at this age to step out of line or to flout "peer-group norms." Such is the widely held view of experts who have studied the behaviors and attitudes of children.[69] This is also

-----

the morning exercises after excusal was made available through amendment of the statute:

"We originally objected to our children being exposed to the reading of the King James version of the Bible . . . and under those conditions we would have theoretically liked to have had the children excused. But we felt that the penalty of having our children labelled as 'odd balls' before their teachers and classmates every day in the year was even less satisfactory than the other problem. . . .

"The children, the classmates of Roger and Donna are very liable to label and lump all particular religious difference or religious objections as atheism, particularly, today the word 'atheism' is so often tied to atheistic communism, and atheism has very bad connotations in the minds of children and many adults today."

A recent opinion of the Attorney General of California gave as one reason for finding devotional exercises unconstitutional the likelihood that "[c]hildren forced by conscience to leave the room during such exercises would be placed in a position inferior to that of students adhering to the State-endorsed religion." 25 Cal. Op. Atty. Gen. 316, 319 (1955). Other views on this question, and possible effects of the excusal procedure, are summarized in Rosenfield, Separation of Church and State in the Public Schools, 22 U. of Pitt. L. Rev. 561, 581–585 (1961); Note, Separation of Church and State: Religious Exercises in the Schools, 31 U. of Cinc. L. Rev. 408, 416 (1962); Note, 62 W. Va. L. Rev. 353, 358 (1960).

[69] Extensive testimony by behavioral scientists concerning the effect of similar practices upon children's attitudes and behaviors is discussed in *Tudor* v. *Board of Education*, 14 N. J. 31, 50–52, 100 A. 2d 857, 867–868. See also Choper, Religion in the Public Schools:

the basis of Mr. Justice Frankfurter's answer to a similar contention made in the *McCollum* case:

> "That a child is offered an alternative may reduce the constraint; it does not eliminate the operation of

---

A Proposed Constitutional Standard, 47 Minn. L. Rev. 329, 344 (1963). There appear to be no reported experiments which bear directly upon the question under consideration. There have, however, been numerous experiments which indicate the susceptibility of school children to peer-group pressures, especially where important group norms and values are involved. See, *e. g.*, Berenda, The Influence of the Group on the Judgments of Children (1950), 26–33; Argyle, Social Pressure in Public and Private Situations, 54 J. Abnormal & Social Psych. 172 (1957); cf. Rhine, The Effect of Peer Group Influence Upon Concept-Attitude Development and Change, 51 J. Social Psych. 173 (1960); French, Morrison and Levinger, Coercive Power and Forces Affecting Conformity, 61 J. Abnormal and Social Psych. 93 (1960). For a recent and important experimental study of the susceptibility of students to various factors in the school environment, see Zander, Curtis and Rosenfeld, The Influence of Teachers and Peers on Aspirations of Youth (U. S. Office of Education Cooperative Research Project No. 451, 1961), 24–25, 78–79. It is also apparent that the susceptibility of school children to prestige suggestion and social influence within the school environment varies inversely with the age, grade level, and consequent degree of sophistication, of the child, see Patel and Gordon, Some Personal and Situational Determinants of Yielding to Influence, 61 J. Abnormal and Social Psych. 411, 417 (1960).

Experimental findings also shed some light upon the probable effectiveness of a provision for excusal when, as is usually the case, the percentage of the class wishing not to participate in the exercises is very small. It has been demonstrated, for example, that the inclination even of adults to depart or dissent overtly from strong group norms varies proportionately with the size of the dissenting group— that is, inversely with the apparent or perceived strength of the norm itself—and is markedly slighter in the case of the sole or isolated dissenter. See, *e. g.*, Asch, Studies of Independence and Conformity: I. A Minority of One Against a Unanimous Majority (Psych. Monographs No. 416, 1956), 69–70; Asch, Effects of Group Pressure upon the Modification and Distortion of Judgments, in Cartwright and Zander, Group Dynamics (2d ed. 1960), 189–199; Luchins and

influence by the school in matters sacred to conscience and outside the school's domain. The law of imitation operates, and non-conformity is not an outstanding characteristic of children. The result is an obvious pressure upon children to attend." 333 U. S., at 227.

Also apposite is the answer given more than 70 years ago by the Supreme Court of Wisconsin to the argument that an excusal provision saved a public school devotional exercise from constitutional invalidation:

". . . the excluded pupil tends to lose caste with his fellows, and is liable to be regarded with aversion, and subjected to reproach and insult. But it is a sufficient refutation of the argument that the practice in question tends to destroy the equality of the pupils which the constitution seeks to establish and protect, and puts a portion of them to serious disadvantage in many ways with respect to others." *State ex rel. Weiss* v. *District Board of School District No. 8,* 76 Wis. 177, 200, 44 N. W. 967, 975.

And 50 years ago a like answer was offered by the Louisiana Supreme Court:

"Under such circumstances, the children would be excused from the opening exercises because of their religious beliefs. And excusing such children on religious grounds, although the number excused might be very small, would be a distinct preference in favor of the religious beliefs of the majority, and would work a discrimination against those who were excused. The exclusion of a pupil under such cir-

Luchins, On Conformity With True and False Communications, 42 J. Social Psych. 283 (1955). Recent important findings on these questions are summarized in Hare, Handbook of Small Group Research (1962), c. II.

cumstances puts him in a class by himself; it subjects him to a religious stigma; and all because of his religious belief. Equality in public education would be destroyed by such act, under a Constitution which seeks to establish equality and freedom in religious matters." *Herold* v. *Parish Board of School Directors,* 136 La. 1034, 1049–1050, 68 So. 116, 121. See also *Tudor* v. *Board of Education,* 14 N. J. 31, 48–52, 100 A. 2d 857, 867–868; *Brown* v. *Orange County Board of Public Instruction,* 128 So. 2d 181, 185 (Fla. App.).

Speiser v. *Randall* also suggests the answer to a further argument based on the excusal procedure. It has been suggested by the School Board, in *Schempp,* that we ought not pass upon the appellees' constitutional challenge at least until the children have availed themselves of the excusal procedure and found it inadequate to redress their grievances. Were the right to be excused not itself of constitutional stature, I might have some doubt about this issue. But we held in *Speiser* that the constitutional vice of the loyalty oath procedure discharged any obligation to seek the exemption before challenging the constitutionality of the conditions upon which it might have been denied. 357 U. S., at 529. Similarly, we have held that one need not apply for a permit to distribute constitutionally protected literature, *Lovell* v. *Griffin,* 303 U. S. 444, or to deliver a speech, *Thomas* v. *Collins,* 323 U. S. 516, before he may attack the constitutionality of a licensing system of which the defect is patent. Insofar as these cases implicate only questions of establishment, it seems to me that the availability of an excuse is constitutionally irrelevant. Moreover, the excusal procedure seems to me to operate in such a way as to discourage the free exercise of religion on the part of those who might wish to utilize it, thereby rendering it unconstitutional in an additional and quite distinct respect.

To summarize my views concerning the merits of these two cases: The history, the purpose and the operation of the daily prayer recital and Bible reading leave no doubt that these practices standing by themselves constitute an impermissible breach of the Establishment Clause. Such devotional exercises may well serve legitimate nonreligious purposes. To the extent, however, that such purposes are really without religious significance, it has never been demonstrated that secular means would not suffice. Indeed, I would suggest that patriotic or other nonreligious materials might provide adequate substitutes—inadequate only to the extent that the purposes now served are indeed directly or indirectly religious. Under such circumstances, the States may not employ religious means to reach a secular goal unless secular means are wholly unavailing. I therefore agree with the Court that the judgment in *Schempp,* No. 142, must be affirmed, and that in *Murray,* No. 119, must be reversed.

V.

These considerations bring me to a final contention of the school officials in these cases: that the invalidation of the exercises at bar permits this Court no alternative but to declare unconstitutional every vestige, however slight, of cooperation or accommodation between religion and government. I cannot accept that contention. While it is not, of course, appropriate for this Court to decide questions not presently before it, I venture to suggest that religious exercises in the public schools present a unique problem. For not every involvement of religion in public life violates the Establishment Clause. Our decision in these cases does not clearly forecast anything about the constitutionality of other types of interdependence between religious and other public institutions.

Specifically, I believe that the line we must draw between the permissible and the impermissible is one which

accords with history and faithfully reflects the understanding of the Founding Fathers. It is a line which the
Court has consistently sought to mark in its decisions
expounding the religious guarantees of the First Amendment. What the Framers meant to foreclose, and what
our decisions under the Establishment Clause have forbidden, are those involvements of religious with secular
institutions which (a) serve the essentially religious
activities of religious institutions; (b) employ the organs
of government for essentially religious purposes; or (c)
use essentially religious means to serve governmental ends,
where secular means would suffice. When the secular
and religious institutions become involved in such a manner, there inhere in the relationship precisely those dangers—as much to church as to state—which the Framers
feared would subvert religious liberty and the strength of
a system of secular government. On the other hand,
there may be myriad forms of involvements of government with religion which do not import such dangers and
therefore should not in my judgment be deemed to violate
the Establishment Clause. Nothing in the Constitution
compels the organs of government to be blind to what
everyone else perceives—that religious differences among
Americans have important and pervasive implications for
our society. Likewise nothing in the Establishment
Clause forbids the application of legislation having purely
secular ends in such a way as to alleviate burdens upon the
free exercise of an individual's religious beliefs. Surely
the. Framers would never have understood that such a
construction sanctions that involvement which violates
the Establishment Clause. Such a conclusion can be
reached, I would suggest, only by using the words of the
First Amendment to defeat its very purpose.

The line between permissible and impermissible forms
of involvement between government and religion has
already been considered by the lower federal and state

courts. I think a brief survey of certain of these forms of accommodation will reveal that the First Amendment commands not official hostility toward religion, but only a strict neutrality in matters of religion. Moreover, it may serve to suggest that the scope of our holding today is to be measured by the special circumstances under which these cases have arisen, and by the particular dangers to church and state which religious exercises in the public schools present. It may be helpful for purposes of analysis to group these other practices and forms of accommodation into several rough categories.

A. *The Conflict Between Establishment and Free Exercise.*—There are certain practices, conceivably violative of the Establishment Clause, the striking down of which might seriously interfere with certain religious liberties also protected by the First Amendment.[70] Provisions for churches and chaplains at military establishments for those in the armed services may afford one such example.[71]

---

[70] See, on the general problem of conflict and accommodation between the two clauses, Katz, Freedom of Religion and State Neutrality, 20 U. of Chi. L. Rev. 426, 429 (1953); Griswold, Absolute Is In the Dark, 8 Utah L. Rev. 167, 176–179 (1963); Kauper, Church, State and Freedom: A Review, 52 Mich. L. Rev. 829, 833 (1954). One author has suggested that the Establishment and Free Exercise Clauses must be "read as stating a single precept: that government cannot utilize religion as a standard for action or inaction because these clauses, read together as they should be, prohibit classification in terms of religion either to confer a benefit or to impose a burden." Kurland, Religion and the Law (1962), 112. Compare the formula of accommodation embodied in the Australian Constitution, § 116:

"The Commonwealth shall not make any law for establishing any religion, or for imposing any religious observance, or for prohibiting the free exercise of any religion, and no religious test shall be required as a qualification for any office or public trust under the Commonwealth." Essays on the Australian Constitution (Else-Mitchell ed. 1961), 15.

[71] There has been much difference of opinion throughout American history concerning the advisability of furnishing chaplains at government expense. Compare, *e. g.*, Washington's order regarding

The like provision by state and federal governments for chaplains in penal institutions may afford another example.[72] It is argued that such provisions may be assumed to contravene the Establishment Clause, yet be sustained on constitutional grounds as necessary to secure to the members of the Armed Forces and prisoners those rights

chaplains for the Continental Army, July 9, 1776, in 5 Writings of George Washington (Fitzpatrick ed. 1932), 244, with Madison's views on a very similar question, letter to Edward Livingston, July 10, 1822, 9 Writings of James Madison (Hunt ed. 1910), 100–103. Compare also this statement by the Armed Forces Chaplains Board concerning the chaplain's obligation:

"To us has been entrusted the spiritual and moral guidance of the young men and women in the Armed Services of this Country. A chaplain has many duties—yet, first and foremost is that of presenting God to men and women wearing the military uniform. What happens to them while they are in military service has a profound effect on what happens in the community as they resume civilian life. We, as chaplains, must take full cognizance of that fact, and dedicate our work to making them finer, spiritually strengthened citizens." Builders of Faith (U. S. Department of Defense 1955), ii.

It is interesting to compare in this regard an express provision, Article 140, of the Weimar Constitution: "Necessary free time shall be accorded to the members of the armed forces for the fulfilment of their religious duties." McBain and Rogers, The New Constitutions of Europe (1922), 203.

[72] For a discussion of some recent and difficult problems in connection with chaplains and religious exercises in prisons, see, *e. g., Pierce* v. *La Vallee,* 293 F. 2d 233; *In re Ferguson,* 55 Cal. 2d 663, 361 P. 2d 417; *McBride* v. *McCorkle,* 44 N. J. Super. 468, 130 A. 2d 881; *Brown* v. *McGinnis,* 10 N. Y. 2d 531, 180 N. E. 2d 791; discussed in Comment, 62 Col. L. Rev. 1488 (1962); 75 Harv. L. Rev. 837 (1962). Compare Article XVIII of the Hague Convention of 1899:

"Prisoners of war shall enjoy every latitude in the exercise of their religion, including attendance at their own church services, provided only they comply with the regulations for order and police issued by the military authorities." Quoted in Blakely, American State Papers and Related Documents on Freedom in Religion (4th rev. ed. 1949), 313.

of worship guaranteed under the Free Exercise Clause. Since government has deprived such persons of the opportunity to practice their faith at places of their choice, the argument runs, government may, in order to avoid infringing the free exercise guarantees, provide substitutes where it requires such persons to be. Such a principle might support, for example, the constitutionality of draft exemptions for ministers and divinity students,[73] cf. *Selective Draft Law Cases,* 245 U. S. 366, 389–390; of the excusal of children from school on their respective religious holidays; and of the allowance by government of temporary use of public buildings by religious organizations when their own churches have become unavailable because of a disaster or emergency.[74]

Such activities and practices seem distinguishable from the sponsorship of daily Bible reading and prayer recital. For one thing, there is no element of coercion present in the appointment of military or prison chaplains; the soldier or convict who declines the opportunities for worship would not ordinarily subject himself to the sus-

---

[73] Compare generally Sibley and Jacob, Conscription of Conscience: The American State and the Conscientious Objector, 1940–1947 (1952), with Conklin, Conscientious Objector Provisions: A View in the Light of *Torcaso v. Watkins,* 51 Geo. L. J. 252 (1963).

[74] See, *e. g., Southside Estates Baptist Church* v. *Board of Trustees,* 115 So. 2d 697 (Fla.); *Lewis* v. *Mandeville,* 200 Misc. 718, 107 N. Y. S. 2d 856; cf. *School District No. 97* v. *Schmidt,* 128 Colo. 495, 263 P. 2d 581 (temporary loan of school district's custodian to church). A different problem may be presented with respect to the regular use of public school property for religious activities, *State ex rel. Gilbert* v. *Dilley,* 95 Neb. 527, 145 N. W. 999; the erection on public property of a statue of or memorial to an essentially religious figure, *State ex rel. Singelman* v. *Morrison,* 57 So. 2d 238 (La. App.); seasonal displays of a religious character, *Baer* v. *Kolmorgen,* 14 Misc. 2d 1015, 181 N. Y. S. 2d 230; or the performance on public property of a drama or opera based on religious material or carrying a religious message, cf. *County of Los Angeles* v. *Hollinger,* 200 Cal. App. 2d 877, 19 Cal. Rptr. 648.

picion or obloquy of his peers. Of special significance to this distinction is the fact that we are here usually dealing with adults, not with impressionable children as in the public schools. Moreover, the school exercises are not designed to provide the pupils with general opportunities for worship denied them by the legal obligation to attend school. The student's compelled presence in school for five days a week in no way renders the regular religious facilities of the community less accessible to him than they are to others. The situation of the school child is therefore plainly unlike that of the isolated soldier or the prisoner.

The State must be steadfastly neutral in all matters of faith, and neither favor nor inhibit religion. In my view, government cannot sponsor religious exercises in the public schools without jeopardizing that neutrality. On the other hand, hostility, not neutrality, would characterize the refusal to provide chaplains and places of worship for prisoners and soldiers cut off by the State from all civilian opportunities for public communion, the withholding of draft exemptions for ministers and conscientious objectors, or the denial of the temporary use of an empty public building to a congregation whose place of worship has been destroyed by fire or flood. I do not say that government *must* provide chaplains or draft exemptions, or that the courts should intercede if it fails to do so.

B. *Establishment and Exercises in Legislative Bodies.*—The saying of invocational prayers in legislative chambers, state or federal, and the appointment of legislative chaplains, might well represent no involvements of the kind prohibited by the Establishment Clause.[75] Legis-

---

[75] Compare Moulton and Myers, Report on Appointing Chaplains to the Legislature of New York, in Blau, Cornerstones of Religious Freedom in America (1949), 141–156; Comment, 63 Col. L. Rev. 73, 97 (1963).

lators, federal and state, are mature adults who may presumably absent themselves from such public and ceremonial exercises without incurring any penalty, direct or indirect. It may also be significant that, at least in the case of the Congress, Art. I, § 5, of the Constitution makes each House the monitor of the "Rules of its Proceedings" so that it is at least arguable whether such matters present "political questions" the resolution of which is exclusively confided to Congress. See *Baker* v. *Carr,* 369 U. S. 186, 232. Finally, there is the difficult question of who may be heard to challenge such practices. See *Elliott* v. *White,* 23 F. 2d 997.

C. *Non-Devotional Use of the Bible In the Public Schools.*—The holding of the Court today plainly does not foreclose teaching *about* the Holy Scriptures or about the differences between religious sects in classes in literature or history. Indeed, whether or not the Bible is involved, it would be impossible to teach meaningfully many subjects in the social sciences or the humanities without some mention of religion.[76] To what extent, and at what points in the curriculum religious materials should be cited, are matters which the courts ought to entrust very largely to the experienced officials who superintend our Nation's public schools. They are experts in such matters, and we are not. We should heed Mr. Justice Jackson's caveat that any attempt by this

---

[76] A comprehensive survey of the problems raised concerning the role of religion in the secular curriculum is contained in Brown, ed., The Study of Religion in the Public Schools: An Appraisal (1958). See also Katz, Religion and American Constitutions, Lecture at Northwestern University Law School, March 21, 1963, pp. 37–41; Educational Policies Comm'n of the National Education Assn., Moral and Spiritual Values in the Public Schools (1951), 49–80. Compare, for a consideration of similar problems in state-supported colleges and universities, Louisell and Jackson, Religion, Theology, and Public Higher Education, 50 Cal. L. Rev. 751 (1962).

Court to announce curricular standards would be "to decree a uniform, rigid and, if we are consistent, an unchanging standard for countless school boards representing and serving highly localized groups which not only differ from each other but which themselves from time to time change attitudes." *Illinois ex rel. McCollum* v. *Board of Education, supra*, at 237.

We do not, however, in my view usurp the jurisdiction of school administrators by holding as we do today that morning devotional exercises in any form are constitutionally invalid. But there is no occasion now to go further, and anticipate problems we cannot judge with the material now before us. Any attempt to impose rigid limits upon the mention of God or references to the Bible in the classroom would be fraught with dangers. If it should sometime hereafter be shown that in fact religion can play no part in the teaching of a given subject without resurrecting the ghost of the practices we strike down today, it will then be time enough to consider questions we must now defer.

D. *Uniform Tax Exemptions Incidentally Available to Religious Institutions.*—Nothing we hold today questions the propriety of certain tax deductions or exemptions which incidentally benefit churches and religious institutions, along with many secular charities and nonprofit organizations. If religious institutions benefit, it is in spite of rather than because of their religious character. For religious institutions simply share benefits which government makes generally available to educational, charitable, and eleemosynary groups.[77] There is no indication

---

[77] See generally Torpey, Judicial Doctrines of Religious Rights in America (1948), c. VI; Van Alstyne, Tax Exemption of Church Property, 20 Ohio State L. J. 461 (1959); Sutherland, Due Process and Disestablishment, 62 Harv. L. Rev. 1306, 1336–1338 (1949);

that taxing authorities have used such benefits in any way to subsidize worship or foster belief in God. And as among religious beneficiaries, the tax exemption or deduction can be truly nondiscriminatory, available on equal terms to small as well as large religious bodies, to popular and unpopular sects, and to those organizations which reject as well as those which accept a belief in God.[78]

E. *Religious Considerations in Public Welfare Programs.*—Since government may not support or directly aid religious *activities* without violating the Establishment Clause, there might be some doubt whether nondiscriminatory programs of governmental aid may constitutionally include *individuals* who become eligible wholly or partially for religious reasons. For example, it might be suggested that where a State provides unemployment compensation generally to those who are unable to find suitable work, it may not extend such benefits to persons who are unemployed by reason of religious beliefs or practices without thereby establishing the religion to which those persons belong. Therefore, the argument runs, the State may avoid an establishment only by singling out and excluding such persons on the ground that religious beliefs or practices have made them potential beneficiaries. Such a construction would, it seems to me, require government to impose religious discriminations and disabilities, thereby jeopardizing the free exercise of religion, in order to avoid what is thought to constitute an establishment.

The inescapable flaw in the argument, I suggest, is its quite unrealistic view of the aims of the Establishment

---

Louisell and Jackson, Religion, Theology, and Public Higher Education, 50 Cal. L. Rev. 751, 773–780 (1962); 7 De Paul L. Rev. 206 (1958); 58 Col. L. Rev. 417 (1958); 9 Stan. L. Rev. 366 (1957).

[78] See, *e. g., Washington Ethical Society* v. *District of Columbia,* 101 U. S. App. D. C. 371, 249 F. 2d 127; *Fellowship of Humanity* v. *County of Alameda,* 153 Cal. App. 2d 673, 315 P. 2d 394.

Clause. The Framers were not concerned with the effects of certain incidental aids to individual worshippers which come about as byproducts of general and nondiscriminatory welfare programs. If such benefits serve to make easier or less expensive the practice of a particular creed, or of all religions, it can hardly be said that the purpose of the program is in any way religious, or that the consequence of its nondiscriminatory application is to create the forbidden degree of interdependence between secular and sectarian institutions. I cannot therefore accept the suggestion, which seems to me implicit in the argument outlined here, that every judicial or administrative construction which is designed to prevent a public welfare program from abridging the free exercise of religious beliefs, is for that reason *ipso facto* an establishment of religion.

F. *Activities Which, Though Religious in Origin, Have Ceased to Have Religious Meaning.*—As we noted in our *Sunday Law* decisions, nearly every criminal law on the books can be traced to some religious principle or inspiration. But that does not make the present enforcement of the criminal law in any sense an establishment of religion, simply because it accords with widely held religious principles. As we said in *McGowan* v. *Maryland,* 366 U. S. 420, 442, "the 'Establishment' clause does not ban federal or state regulation of conduct whose reason or effect merely happens to coincide or harmonize with the tenets of some or all religions." This rationale suggests that the use of the motto "In God We Trust" on currency, on documents and public buildings and the like may not offend the clause. It is not that the use of those four words can be dismissed as "de minimis"—for I suspect there would be intense opposition to the abandonment of that motto. The truth is that we have simply interwoven the motto so deeply into the fabric of our civil polity that its present use may well not present that type of involvement which the First Amendment prohibits.

This general principle might also serve to insulate the various patriotic exercises and activities used in the public schools and elsewhere which, whatever may have been their origins, no longer have a religious purpose or meaning. The reference to divinity in the revised pledge of allegiance, for example, may merely recognize the historical fact that our Nation was believed to have been founded "under God." Thus reciting the pledge may be no more of a religious exercise than the reading aloud of Lincoln's Gettysburg Address, which contains an allusion to the same historical fact.

The principles which we reaffirm and apply today can hardly be thought novel or radical. They are, in truth, as old as the Republic itself, and have always been as integral a part of the First Amendment as the very words of that charter of religious liberty. No less applicable today than they were when first pronounced a century ago, one year after the very first court decision involving religious exercises in the public schools, are the words of a distinguished Chief Justice of the Commonwealth of Pennsylvania, Jeremiah S. Black:

> "The manifest object of the men who framed the institutions of this country, was to have a *State without religion,* and a *Church without politics*—that is to say, they meant that one should never be used as an engine for any purpose of the other, and that no man's rights in one should be tested by his opinions about the other. As the Church takes no note of men's political differences, so the State looks with equal eye on all the modes of religious faith. . . . Our fathers seem to have been perfectly sincere in

their belief that the members of the Church would be more patriotic, and the citizens of the State more religious, by keeping their respective functions entirely separate." Essay on Religious Liberty, in Black, ed., Essays and Speeches of Jeremiah S. Black (1886), 53.

SUPREME COURT OF THE UNITED STATES

Nos. 142 AND 119.—OCTOBER TERM, 1962.

School District of Abington Township, Pennsylvania, et al., Appellants, 142 *v.* Edward Lewis Schempp et al.	On Appeal From the United States District Court for the Eastern District of Pennsylvania.
William J. Murray III, etc., et al., Petitioners, 119 *v.* John N. Curlett, President, et al., Individually, and Constituting the Board of School Commissioners of Baltimore City.	On Writ of Certiorari to the Court of Appeals of Maryland.

[June 17, 1963.]

MR. JUSTICE GOLDBERG, with whom MR. JUSTICE HARLAN joins, concurring.

As is apparent from the opinions filed today, delineation of the constitutionally permissible relationship between religion and government is a most difficult and sensitive task, calling for the careful exercise of both judicial and public judgment and restraint. The considerations which lead the Court today to interdict the clearly religious practices presented in these cases are to me wholly compelling; I have no doubt as to the propriety of the decision and therefore join the opinion and judgment of the Court. The singular sensitivity and concern which surround both the legal and practical judgments involved impel me, however, to add a few words in further explication, while at the same time avoiding repetition of the carefully and ably framed examination of history and authority by my Brethren.

The First Amendment's guarantees, as applied to the states through the Fourteenth Amendment, foreclose not only laws "respecting an establishment of religion" but also those "prohibiting the free exercise thereof." These two proscriptions are to be read together, and in light of the single end which they are designed to serve. The basic purpose of the First Amendment is to promote and assure the fullest possible scope of religious liberty and tolerance for all and to nurture the conditions which secure the best hope of attainment of that end.

The fullest realization of true religious liberty requires that government neither engage in nor compel religious practices, that it effect no favoritism among sects or between religion and nonreligion, and that it work deterrence of no religious belief. But devotion even to these simply stated objectives presents no easy course, for the unavoidable accommodations necessary to achieve the maximum enjoyment of each and all of them are often difficult of discernment. There is for me no simple and clear measure which by precise application can readily and invariably demark the permissible from the impermissible.

It is said, and I agree, that the attitude of the state toward religion must be one of neutrality. But untutored devotion to the concept of neutrality can lead to invocation or approval of results which partake not simply of that noninterference and noninvolvement with the religious which the Constitution commands, but of a brooding and pervasive devotion to the secular and a passive, or even active, hostility to the religious. Such results are not only not compelled by the Constitution, but, it seems to me, are prohibited by it.

Neither the state nor this Court can or should ignore the significance of the fact that a vast portion of our people believe in and worship God and that many of our legal, political and personal values derive historically from religious teachings. Government must inevitably take cognizance of the existence of religion and, indeed, under certain circumstances the First Amendment may require that it do so. And it seems clear to me from the opinions in the present and past cases that the Court would recognize the propriety of providing military chaplains and of the teaching *about* religion, as distinguished from the teaching *of* religion, in the public schools. The examples could readily be multiplied, for both the required and the permissible accommodations between state and church frame the relation as one free of hostility or favor and productive of religious and political harmony, but without undue involvement of one in the concerns or practices of the other. To be sure, the judgment in each case is a delicate one, but it must be made if we are to do loyal service as judges to the ultimate First Amendment objective of religious liberty.

The practices here involved do not fall within any sensible or acceptable concept of compelled or permitted accommodation and involve the state so significantly and directly in the realm of the sectarian as to give rise to those very divisive influences and inhibitions of freedom which both religion clauses of the First Amendment preclude. The state has ordained and has utilized its facilities to engage in unmistakably religious exercises—the devotional reading and recitation of the Holy Bible—in a manner having substantial and significant import and impact. That it has selected, rather than written, a particular devotional liturgy seems to me without constitutional import. The pervasive religiosity and direct governmental involvement inhering in the prescription of prayer and Bible reading in the public schools, during and as part of the curricular day, involving young impressionable children whose school attendance is statutorily compelled, and utilizing the prestige, power, and influence of school administration, staff, and authority, cannot realistically be termed simply accommodation, and must fall within the interdiction of the First Amendment. I find nothing in the opinion of the Court which says more than this. And, of course, today's decision does not mean that all incidents of government which import of the religious are therefore and without more banned by the strictures of the Establishment Clause. As the Court declared only last Term in *Engel* v. *Vitale*, 370 U. S. 421, 435, n. 21:

> "There is of course nothing in the decision reached here that is inconsistent with the fact that school children and others are officially encouraged to express love for our country by reciting historical documents such as the Declaration of Independence which contain references to the Deity or by singing officially espoused anthems which include the composer's professions of faith in a Supreme Being, or with the fact that there are many manifestations in our public life of belief in God. Such patriotic or ceremonial occasions bear no true resemblance to the unquestioned religious exercise that the State . . . has sponsored in this instance."

The First Amendment does not prohibit practices which by any realistic measure create none of the dangers which it is designed to prevent and which do not so directly or substantially involve the state in religious exercises or in the favoring of religion as to have meaningful and practical impact. It is of course true that great consequences can grow from small beginnings, but the measure of constitutional adjudication is the ability and willingness to distinguish between real threat and mere shadow.

SUPREME COURT OF THE UNITED STATES

School District of Abington Township, Pennsylvania, et al., Appellants, 142 *v.* Edward Lewis Schempp et al.	On Appeal From the United States District Court for the Eastern District of Pennsylvania.
William J. Murray III, etc., et al., Petitioners, 119 *v.* John N. Curlett, President, et al., Individually, and Constituting the Board of School Commissioners of Baltimore City.	On Writ of Certiorari to the Court of Appeals of Maryland.

[June 17, 1963.]

MR. JUSTICE STEWART, dissenting.

I think the records in the two cases before us are so fundamentally deficient as to make impossible an informed or responsible determination of the constitutional issues presented. Specifically, I cannot agree that on these records we can say that the Establishment Clause has necessarily been violated.[1] But I think there exist serious questions under both that provision and the Free Exercise Clause—insofar as each is imbedded in the Fourteenth Amendment—which require the remand of these cases for the taking of additional evidence.

---

[1] It is instructive, in this connection, to examine the complaints in the two cases before us. Neither complaint attacks the challenged practices as "establishments." What both allege as the basis for their causes of actions are, rather, violations of religious liberty.

I.

The First Amendment declares that "Congress shall make no law respecting an establishment of religion, or prohibiting the free exercise thereof . . . ." It is, I think, a fallacious oversimplification to regard these two provisions as establishing a single constitutional standard of "separation of church and state," which can be mechanically applied in every case to delineate the required boundaries between government and religion. We err in the first place if we do not recognize, as a matter of history and as a matter of the imperatives of our free society, that religion and government must necessarily interact in countless ways. Secondly, the fact is that while in many contexts the Establishment Clause and the Free Exercise Clause fully complement each other, there are areas in which a doctrinaire reading of the Establishment Clause leads to irreconcilable conflict with the Free Exercise Clause.

A single obvious example should suffice to make the point. Spending federal funds to employ chaplains for the armed forces might be said to violate the Establishment Clause. Yet a lonely soldier stationed at some faraway outpost could surely complain that a government which did *not* provide him the opportunity for pastoral guidance was affirmatively prohibiting the free exercise of his religion. And such examples could readily be multiplied. The short of the matter is simply that the two relevant clauses of the First Amendment cannot accurately be reflected in a sterile metaphor which by its very nature may distort rather than illumine the problems involved in a particular case. Cf. *Sherbert* v. *Verner, post,* p. ——.

II.

As a matter of history, the First Amendment was adopted solely as a limitation upon the newly created National Government. The events leading to its adoption strongly suggest that the Establishment Clause was primarily an attempt to insure that Congress not only would be powerless to establish a national church, but would also be unable to interfere with existing state establishments. See *McGowan* v. *Maryland,* 366 U. S. 420, 440–441. Each State was left free to go its own way and pursue its own policy with respect to religion. Thus Virginia from the beginning pursued a policy of disestablishmentarianism. Massachusetts, by contrast, had an established church until well into the nineteenth century.

So matters stood until the adoption of the Fourteenth Amendment, or more accurately, until this Court's decision in *Cantwell* v. *Connecticut,* in 1940. 310 U. S. 296. In that case the Court said: "The First Amendment declares that Congress shall make no law respecting an establishment of religion or prohibiting the free exercise thereof. The Fourteenth Amendment has rendered the legislatures of the states as incompetent as Congress to enact such laws." [2]

I accept without question that the liberty guaranteed by the Fourteenth Amendment against impairment by the States embraces in full the right of free exercise of religion protected by the First Amendment, and I yield to no one in my conception of the breadth of that freedom. See *Braunfeld* v. *Brown,* 366 U. S. 599, 616 (dissenting opinion). I accept too the proposition that the Fourteenth Amendment has somehow absorbed the Establishment Clause, although it is not without irony that a constitutional provision evidently designed to leave the States free to go their own way should now have become a restriction upon their autonomy. But I cannot agree with what seems to me the insensitive definition of the Establishment Clause contained in the Court's opinion, nor

---

[2] 310 U. S., at 303. The Court's statement as to the Establishment Clause in *Cantwell* was dictum. The case was decided on free exercise grounds.

with the different but, I think, equally mechanistic definitions contained in the separate opinions which have been filed.

III.

Since the *Cantwell* pronouncement in 1940, this Court has only twice held invalid state laws on the ground that they were laws "respecting an establishment of religion" in violation of the Fourteenth Amendment. *McCollum* v. *Board of Education,* 333 U. S. 203; *Engel* v. *Vitale,* 370 U. S. 421. On the other hand, the Court has upheld against such a challenge laws establishing Sunday as a compulsory day of rest, *McGowan* v. *Maryland,* 366 U. S. 420, and a law authorizing reimbursement from public funds for the transportation of parochial school pupils. *Everson* v. *Board of Education,* 330 U. S. 1.

Unlike other First Amendment guarantees, there is an inherent limitation upon the applicability of the Establishment Clause's ban on state support to religion. That limitation was succinctly put in *Everson* v. *Board of Education,* 330 U. S. 1, 18: "State power is no more to be used so as to handicap religions than it is to favor them." [3] And in a later case, this Court recognized that the limitation was one which was itself compelled by the free exercise guarantee. "To hold that a state cannot consistently with the First and Fourteenth Amendments utilize its public school system to aid any or all religious faiths or sects in the dissemination of their doctrines and ideals does not . . . manifest a governmental hostility to reli-

---

[3] See also, in this connection, *Zorach* v. *Clauson,* 343 U. S. 306, 314: "Government may not finance religious groups nor undertake religious instruction nor blend secular and sectarian education nor use secular institutions to force one or some religion on any person. But we find no constitutional requirement which makes it necessary for government to be hostile to religion and to throw its weight against efforts to widen the effective scope of religious influence."

gion or religious teaching. A manifestation of such hostility would be at war with our national tradition as embodied in the First Amendment's guaranty of the free exercise of religion." *McCollum* v. *Board of Education,* 333 U. S. 203, 211–212.

That the central value embodied in the First Amendment—and, more particularly, in the guarantee of "liberty" contained in the Fourteenth—is the safeguarding of an individual's right to free exercise of his religion has been consistently recognized. Thus, in the case of *Hamilton* v. *Regents,* 293 U. S. 245, 265, Mr. Justice Cardozo, concurring, assumed that it was ". . . *the religious liberty* protected by the First Amendment against invasion by the nation [which] is protected by the Fourteenth Amendment against invasion by the states." (Emphasis added.) And in *Cantwell* v. *Connecticut, supra,* the purpose of those guarantees was described in the following terms: "On the one hand, it forestalls compulsion by law of the acceptance of any creed or the practice of any form of worship. Freedom of conscience and freedom to adhere to such religious organization or form of worship as the individual may choose cannot be restricted by law. On the other hand, it safeguards the free exercise of the chosen form of religion." 310 U. S., at 303.

It is this concept of constitutional protection embodied in our decisions which makes the cases before us such difficult ones for me. For there is involved in these cases a substantial free exercise claim on the part of those who affirmatively desire to have their children's school day open with the reading of passages from the Bible.

It has become accepted that the decision in *Pierce* v. *Society of Sisters,* 268 U. S. 510, upholding the right of parents to send their children to nonpublic schools, was ultimately based upon the recognition of the validity of the free exercise claim involved in that situation. It might be argued here that parents who wanted their children to be exposed to religious influences in school could, under *Pierce,* send their children to private or parochial schools. But the consideration which renders this contention too facile to be determinative has already been recognized by the Court: "Freedom of speech, freedom of the press, freedom of religion are available to all, not merely to those who can pay their own way." *Murdock* v. *Pennsylvania,* 319 U. S. 105, 111.

It might also be argued that parents who want their children exposed to religious influences can adequately fulfill that wish off school property and outside school time. With all its surface persuasiveness, however, this argument seriously misconceives the basic constitutional justification for permitting the exercises at issue in these cases. For a compulsory state educational system so structures a child's life that if religious exercises are held to be an impermissible activity in schools, religion is placed at an artificial and state-created disadvantage. Viewed in this light, permission of such exercises for those who want them is necessary if the schools are truly to be neutral in the matter of religion. And a refusal to permit religious exercises thus is seen, not as the realization of state neutrality, but rather as the establishment of a religion of secularism, or at the least, as government support of the beliefs of those who think that religious exercises should be conducted only in private.

What seems to me to be of paramount importance, then, is recognition of the fact that the claim advanced here in favor of Bible reading is sufficiently substantial to make simple reference to the constitutional phrase "establishment of religion" as inadequate an analysis of the cases before us as the ritualistic invocation of the nonconstitutional phrase "separation of church and state." What these cases compel, rather, is an analysis of just what the "neutrality" is which is required by the interplay of the Establishment and Free Exercise Clauses of the First Amendment, as imbedded in the Fourteenth.

IV.

Our decisions make clear that there is no constitutional bar to the use of government property for religious purposes. On the contrary, this Court has consistently held that the discriminatory barring of religious groups from public property is itself a violation of First and Fourteenth Amendment guarantees. *Fowler* v. *Rhode Island,* 345 U. S. 67; *Niemotko* v. *Maryland,* 340 U. S. 268. A different standard has been applied to public school property, because of the coercive effect which the use by religious sects of a compulsory school system would necessarily have upon the children involved. *McCollum* v. *Board of Education,* 333 U. S. 203. But insofar as the *McCollum* decision rests on the Establishment rather than the Free Exercise Clause, it is clear that its effect is limited to religious instruction—to government support of proselytizing activities of religious sects by throwing the weight of secular authority behind the dissemination of religious tenets.[4]

The dangers both to government and to religion inherent in official support of instruction in the tenets of various religious sects are absent in the present cases, which involve only a reading from the Bible unaccompanied by comments which might otherwise constitute instruction. Indeed, since, from all that appears in either record, any teacher who does not wish to do so is free

---

[4] "This is beyond all question a utilization of the tax-established and tax-supported public school system to aid religious groups *to spread their faith.*" *McCollum* v. *Board of Education,* 333 U. S. 203, 210. (Emphasis added.)

not to participate,[5] it cannot even be contended that some infinitesimal part of the salaries paid by the State are made contingent upon the performance of a religious function.

In the absence of evidence that the legislature or school board intended to prohibit local schools from substituting a different set of readings where parents requested such a change, we should not assume that the provisions before us—as actually administered—may not be construed simply as authorizing religious exercises, nor that the designations may not be treated simply as indications of the promulgating body's view as to the community's preference. We are under a duty to interpret these provisions so as to render them constitutional if reasonably possible. Compare *Two Guys* v. *McGinley*, 366 U. S. 582, 592–595; *Everson* v. *Board of Education*, 330 U. S. 1, 4, and n. 2. In the *Schempp* case there is evidence which indicates that variations were in fact permitted by the very school there involved, and that further variations were not introduced only because of the absence of requests from parents. And in the *Murray* case the Baltimore rule itself contains a provision permitting another version of the Bible to be substituted for the King James version.

If the provisions are not so construed, I think that their validity under the Establishment Clause would be extremely doubtful, because of the designation of a particular religious book and a denominational prayer. But since, even if the provisions are construed as I believe they must be, I think that the cases before us must be re-

---

[5] The Pennsylvania statute was specifically amended to remove the compulsion upon teachers. Act of December 17, 1959, P. L. 1928, 24 Purdon's Pa. Stat. Ann. § 15–1516. Since the Maryland case is here on a demurrer, the issue of whether or not a teacher could be dismissed for refusal to participate seems, among many others, never to have been raised.

manded for further evidence on other issues—thus affording the plaintiffs an opportunity to prove that local variations are not in fact permitted—I shall for the balance of this dissenting opinion treat the provisions before us as making the variety and content of the exercises, as well as a choice as to their implementation, matters which ultimately reflect the concensus of each local school community. In the absence of coercion upon those who do not wish to participate—because they hold less strong beliefs, other beliefs, or no beliefs at all— such provisions cannot, in my view, be held to represent the type of support of religion barred by the Establishment Clause. For the only support which such rules provide for religion is the withholding of state hostility—a simple acknowledgment on the part of secular authorities that the Constitution does not require extirpation of all expression of religious belief.

V.

I have said that these provisions authorizing religious exercises are properly to be regarded as measures making possible the free exercise of religion. But it is important to stress that, strictly speaking, what is at issue here is a privilege rather than a right. In other words, the question presented is not whether exercises such as those at issue here are constitutionally compelled, but rather whether they are constitutionally invalid. And that issue, in my view, turns on the question of coercion.

It is clear that the dangers of coercion involved in the holding of religious exercises in a schoolroom differ qualitatively from those presented by the use of similar exercises or affirmations in ceremonies attended by adults. Even as to children, however, the duty laid upon government in connection with religious exercises in the public schools is that of refraining from so structuring the school environment as to put any kind of pressure on a child to participate in those exercises; it is not that of providing an atmosphere in which children are kept scrupulously insulated from any awareness that some of their fellows may want to open the school day with prayer, or of the fact that there exist in our pluralistic society differences of religious belief.

These are not, it must be stressed, cases like *Brown* v. *Board of Education,* 347 U. S. 483, in which this Court held that, in the sphere of public education, the Fourteenth Amendment's guarantee of equal protection of the laws required that race not be treated as a relevant factor. A segregated school system is not invalid because its operation is coercive; it is invalid simply because our Constitution presupposes that men are created equal, and that therefore racial differences cannot provide a valid basis for governmental action. Accommodation of religious differences on the part of the State, however, is not only permitted but required by that same Constitution.

The governmental neutrality which the First and Fourteenth Amendments require in the cases before us, in other words, is the extension of even-handed treatment to all who believe, doubt, or disbelieve—a refusal on the part of the State to weight the scales of private choice. In these cases, therefore, what is involved is not state action based on impermissible categories, but rather an attempt by the State to accommodate those differences which the existence in our society of a variety of religious beliefs make inevitable. The Constitution requires that such efforts be struck down only if they are proven to entail the use of the secular authority of government to coerce a preference among such beliefs.

It may well be, as has been argued to us, that even the supposed benefits to be derived from noncoercive religious exercises in public schools are incommensurate with the administrative problems which they would create. The choice involved, however, is one for each local community and its school board, and not for this Court. For, as I have said, religious exercises are not constitutionally invalid if they simply reflect differences which exist in the society from which the school draws its pupils. They become constitutionally invalid only if their administration places the sanction of secular authority behind one or more particular religious or irreligious beliefs.

To be specific, it seems to me clear that certain types of exercises would present situations in which no possibility of coercion on the part of secular officials could be claimed to exist. Thus, if such exercises were held either before or after the official school day, or if the school schedule were such that participation were merely one among a number of desirable alternatives,[6] it could hardly be contended that the exercises did anything more than to provide an opportunity for the voluntary expression of religious belief. On the other hand, a law which provided for religious exercises during the school day and which contained no excusal provision would obviously be unconstitutionally coercive upon those who did not wish to participate. And even under a law containing an excusal provision, if the exercises were held during the school day, and no equally desirable alternative were provided by the school authorities, the likelihood that children might be under at least some psychological compulsion to participate would be great. In a case such as the latter, however, I think we would err if we *assumed* such coercion in the absence of any evidence.[7]

---

[6] See, *e. g.*, the description of a plan permitting religious instruction off school property contained in *McCollum* v. *Board of Education,* 333 U. S. 203, 224 (separate opinion of Mr. Justice Frankfurter).

[7] Cf. "The task of separating the secular from the religious in education is one of magnitude, intricacy and delicacy. To lay down a sweeping constitutional doctrine as demanded by complainant and apparently approved by the Court, applicable alike to all school

VI.

Viewed in this light, it seems to me clear that the records in both of the cases before us are wholly inadequate to support an informed or responsible decision. Both cases involve provisions which explicitly permit any student who wishes, to be excused from participation in the exercises. There is no evidence in either case as to whether there would exist any coercion of any kind upon a student who did not want to participate. No evidence at all was adduced in the *Murray* case, because it was decided upon a demurrer. All that we have in that case, therefore, is the conclusory language of a pleading. While such conclusory allegations are acceptable for procedural purposes, I think that the nature of the constitutional problem involved here clearly demands that no decision be made except upon evidence. In the *Schempp* case the record shows no more than a subjective prophecy by a parent of what he thought would happen if a request were made to be excused from participation in the exercises under the amended statute. No such request was ever made, and there is no evidence whatever as to what might or would actually happen, nor of what administrative arrangements the school actually might or could make to free from pressure of any kind those who do not want to participate in the exercises. There were no District Court findings on this issue, since

---

boards of the nation, . . . is to decree a uniform, rigid and, if we are consistent, an unchanging standard for countless school boards representing and serving highly localized groups which not only differ from each other but which themselves from time to time change attitudes. It seems to me that to do so is to allow zeal for our own ideas of what is good in public instruction to induce us to accept the role of a super board of education for every school district in the nation." *McCollum* v. *Board of Education*, 333 U. S. 203, 237 (concurring opinion of Mr. Justice Jackson).

the case under the amended statute was decided exclusively on Establishment Clause grounds. 201 F. Supp. 815.

What our Constitution indispensably protects is the freedom of each of us, be he Jew or Agnostic, Christian or Atheist, Buddhist or Freethinker, to believe or disbelieve, to worship or not worship, to pray or keep silent, according to his own conscience, uncoerced and unrestrained by government. It is conceivable that these school boards, or even all school boards, might eventually find it impossible to administer a system of religious exercises during school hours in such a way as to meet this constitutional standard—in such a way as completely to free from any kind of official coercion those who do not affirmatively want to participate.[8] But I think we must not assume that school boards so lack the qualities of inventiveness and good will as to make impossible the achievement of that goal.

I would remand both cases for further hearings.

---

[8] For example, if the record in the *Schempp* case contained proof (rather than mere prophecy) that the timing of morning announcements by the school was such as to handicap children who did not want to listen to the Bible reading, or that the excusal provision was so administered as to carry any overtones of social inferiority, then impermissible coercion would clearly exist.

AN EARLIER DECISION

In order to provide a fully-rounded picture of the Supreme Court's present position on religious practices in the public schools, we now reprint its decision in the case of *Engel v. Vitale,* which was handed down almost exactly a year before the Bible-reading verdict and was a forerunner of the latter decision.

In *Engel v. Vitale,* the Court passed upon the constitutionality of a 22-word "nondenominational" prayer, which had been composed for use in the schools of New York by the Board of Regents of that state. As in the Bible-reading cases, the Court held the religious practice to be violative of the First and Fourteenth Amendments— again with only a single member of the Court, Mr. Justice Stewart, dissenting from the majority opinion.

Because the dissenting views of Mr. Justice Stewart were set forth at greater length in the Bible-reading cases, we do not reprint his dissent in the *Engel* case. The majority opinion, however, was this time written by Mr. Justice Black; and because it adds important considerations to the reasoning that supported the later Bible-reading decision, we now reprint it in full, omitting only certain technical footnotes.

SUPREME COURT OF THE UNITED STATES

No. 468.—October Term, 1961.

Steven I. Engel et al., Petitioners, *v.* William J. Vitale, Jr., et al.

On Writ of Certiorari to the Court of Appeals of New York.

[June 25, 1962.]

Mr. Justice Black delivered the opinion of the Court.

The respondent Board of Education of Union Free School District No. 9, New Hyde Park, New York, acting in its official capacity under state law, directed the School District's principal to cause the following prayer to be said aloud by each class in the presence of a teacher at the beginning of each school day:

> "Almighty God, we acknowledge our dependence upon Thee, and we beg Thy blessings upon us, our parents, our teachers and our country."

This daily procedure was adopted on the recommendation of the State Board of Regents, a governmental agency created by the State Constitution to which the New York Legislature has granted broad supervisory, executive, and legislative powers over the State's public school system.[1] These state officials composed the prayer which they recommended and published as a part of their "Statement on Moral and Spiritual Training in the Schools," saying: "We believe that this Statement will be subscribed to by all men and women of good will, and we call upon all of them to aid in giving life to our program."

---

[1] See New York Constitution, Art. V, § 4; New York Education Law, §§ 101, 120 *et seq.*, 202, 214–219, 224, 245 *et seq.*, 704, and 801 *et seq.*

Shortly after the practice of reciting the Regents' prayer was adopted by the School District, the parents of ten pupils brought this action in a New York State Court insisting that use of this official prayer in the public schools was contrary to the beliefs, religions, or religious practices of both themselves and their children. Among other things, these parents challenged the constitutionality of both the state law authorizing the School District to direct the use of prayer in public schools and the School District's regulation ordering the recitation of this particular prayer on the ground that these actions of official governmental agencies violate that part of the First Amendment of the Federal Constitution which commands that "Congress shall make no law respecting an establishment of religion"—a command which was "made applicable to the State of New York by the Fourteenth Amendment of the said Constitution." The New York Court of Appeals, over the dissents of Judges Dye and Fuld, sustained an order of the lower state courts which had upheld the power of New York to use the Regents' prayer as a part of the daily procedures of its public schools so long as the schools did not compel any pupil to join in the prayer over his or his parents' objection.[2] We granted certiorari to review this important decision involving rights protected by the First and Fourteenth Amendments.[3]

We think that by using its public school system to encourage recitation of the Regents' prayer, the State of New York has adopted a practice wholly inconsistent with the Establishment Clause. There can, of course, be no doubt that New York's program of daily classroom invocation of God's blessings as prescribed in the Regents' prayer is a religious activity. It is a solemn avowal of divine faith and supplication for the blessings of the Almighty. The nature of such a prayer has always been religious, none of the respondents has denied this and the trial court expressly so found:

> "The religious nature of prayer was recognized by Jefferson and has been concurred in by theological writers, the United States Supreme Court and State courts and administrative officials, including New York's Commissioner of Education. A committee of the New York Legislature has agreed.

> "The Board of Regents as *amicus curiae*, the respondents and intervenors all concede the religious nature of prayer, but seek to distinguish this prayer because it is based on our spiritual heritage. . . ." [4]

The petitioners contend among other things that the state laws requiring or permitting use of the Regents' prayer must be struck down as a violation of the Establishment Clause because that prayer was composed by governmental officials as a part of a governmental program to further religious beliefs. For this reason, petitioners argue, the State's use of the Regents' prayer in its public school system breaches the constitutional wall of separation between Church and State. We agree with that contention since we think that the constitutional prohibition against laws respecting an establishment of religion must at least mean that in this country it is no part of the business of government to compose official prayers for any group of the American people to recite as a part of a religious program carried on by government.

It is a matter of history that this very practice of establishing governmentally composed prayers for religious services was one of the reasons which caused many of our early colonists to leave England and seek religious freedom in America. The Book of Common Prayer, which was created under governmental direction and which was approved by Acts of Parliament in 1548 and 1549,[5] set out in minute detail the accepted form and content of prayer and other religious ceremonies to be used in the established, tax-supported Church of Eng-

land.[6]   The controversies over the Book and what should
be its content repeatedly threatened to disrupt the peace
of that country as the accepted forms of prayer in the
established church changed with the views of the particular ruler that happened to be in control at the time.[7]
Powerful groups representing some of the varying religious views of the people struggled among themselves to
impress their particular views upon the Government and
obtain amendments of the Book more suitable to their
respective notions of how religious services should be conducted in order that the official religious establishment
would advance their particular religious beliefs.[8]   Other
groups, lacking the necessary political power to influence
the Government on the matter, decided to leave England
and its established church and seek freedom in America
from England's governmentally ordained and supported
religion.

It is an unfortunate fact of history that when some of
the very groups which had most strenuously opposed the
established Church of England found themselves sufficiently in control of colonial governments in this country
to write their own prayers into law, they passed laws making their own religion the official religion of their respective colonies.[9]   Indeed, as late as the time of the Revolutionary War, there were established churches in at least
eight of the thirteen former colonies and established religions in at least four of the other five.[10]   But the successful Revolution against English political domination was
shortly followed by intense opposition to the practice of
establishing religion by law.   This opposition crystallized
rapidly into an effective political force in Virginia where
the minority religious groups such as Presbyterians, Lutherans, Quakers and Baptists had gained such strength
that the adherents to the established Episcopal Church
were actually a minority themselves. In 1785–1786,
those opposed to the established Church, led by James
Madison and Thomas Jefferson, who, though themselves

not members of any of these dissenting religious groups, opposed all religious establishments by law on grounds of principle, obtained the enactment of the famous "Virginia Bill for Religious Liberty" by which all religious groups were placed on an equal footing so far as the State was concerned.[11]   Similar though less far-reaching legislation was being considered and passed in other States.[12]

By the time of the adoption of the Constitution, our history shows that there was a widespread awareness among many Americans of the dangers of a union of Church and State.   These people knew, some of them from bitter personal experience, that one of the greatest dangers to the freedom of the individual to worship in his own way lay in the Government's placing its official stamp of approval upon one particular kind of prayer or one particular form of religious services.   They knew the anguish, hardship and bitter strife that could come when zealous religious groups struggled with one another to obtain the Government's stamp of approval from each King, Queen, or Protector that came to temporary power. The Constitution was intended to avert a part of this danger by leaving the government of this country in the hands of the people rather than in the hands of any monarch.   But this safeguard was not enough.   Our Founders were no more willing to let the content of their prayers and their privilege of praying whenever they pleased be influenced by the ballot box than they were to let these vital matters of personal conscience depend upon the succession of monarchs.   The First Amendment was added to the Constitution to stand as a guarantee that neither the power nor the prestige of the Federal Government would be used to control, support or influence the kinds of prayer the American people can say— that the people's religions must not be subjected to the pressures of government for change each time a new political administration is elected to office.   Under that Amendment's prohibition against governmental establishment of religion, as reinforced by the provisions of the

Fourteenth Amendment, government in this country, be it state or federal, is without power to prescribe by law any particular form of prayer which is to be used as an official prayer in carrying on any program of governmentally sponsored religious activity.

There can be no doubt that New York's state prayer program officially establishes the religious beliefs embodied in the Regents' prayer. The respondents' argument to the contrary, which is largely based upon the contention that the Regents' prayer is "non-denominational" and the fact that the program, as modified and approved by state courts, does not require all pupils to recite the prayer but permits those who wish to do so to remain silent or be excused from the room, ignores the essential nature of the program's constitutional defects. Neither the fact that the prayer may be denominationally neutral, nor the fact that its observance on the part of the students is voluntary can serve to free it from the limitations of the Establishment Clause, as it might from the Free Exercise Clause, of the First Amendment, both of which are operative against the States by virtue of the Fourteenth Amendment. Although these two clauses may in certain instances overlap, they forbid two quite different kinds of governmental encroachment upon religious freedom. The Establishment Clause, unlike the Free Exercise Clause, does not depend upon any showing of direct governmental compulsion and is violated by the enactment of laws which establish an official religion whether those laws operate directly to coerce nonobserving individuals or not. This is not to say, of course, that laws officially prescribing a particular form of religious worship do not involve coercion of such individuals. When the power, prestige and financial support of government is placed behind a particular religious belief, the indirect coercive pressure upon religious minorities to conform to the prevailing officially approved religion is plain. But the purposes underlying the Establishment Clause

go much further than that. Its first and most immediate purpose rested on the belief that a union of government and religion tends to destroy government and to
degrade religion. The history of governmentally established religion, both in England and in this country,
showed that whenever government had allied itself with
one particular form of religion, the inevitable result had
been that it had incurred the hatred, disrespect and even
contempt of those who held contrary beliefs.[13] That same
history showed that many people had lost their respect
for any religion that had relied upon the support of government to spread its faith.[14] The Establishment Clause
thus stands as an expression of principle on the part of the
Founders of our Constitution that religion is too personal,
too sacred, too holy, to permit its "unhallowed perversion"
by a civil magistrate.[15] Another purpose of the Establishment Clause rested upon an awareness of the historical
fact that governmentally established religions and religious persecutions go hand in hand.[16] The Founders
knew that only a few years after the Book of Common
Prayer became the only accepted form of religious services in the established Church of England, an Act of Uniformity was passed to compel all Englishmen to attend
those services and to make it a criminal offense to conduct
or attend religious gatherings of any other kind [17]—a law
which was consistently flouted by dissenting religious
groups in England and which contributed to widespread
persecutions of people like John Bunyan who persisted in
holding "unlawful [religious] meetings . . . to the great
disturbance and distraction of the good subjects of this
kingdom. . . ." [18] And they knew that similar persecutions had received the sanction of law in several of the
colonies in this country soon after the establishment of
official religions in those colonies.[19] It was in large part
to get completely away from this sort of systematic religious persecution that the Founders brought into being

our Nation, our Constitution, and our Bill of Rights with its prohibition against any governmental establishment of religion.   The New York laws officially prescribing the Regents' prayer are inconsistent with both the purposes of the Establishment Clause and with the Establishment Clause itself.

It has been argued that to apply the Constitution in such a way as to prohibit state laws respecting an establishment of religious services in public schools is to indicate a hostility toward religion or toward prayer. Nothing, of course, could be more wrong.   The history of man is inseparable from the history of religion.   And perhaps it is not too much to say that since the beginning of that history many people have devoutly believed that "More things are wrought by prayer than this world dreams of."   It was doubtless largely due to men who believed this that there grew up a sentiment that caused men to leave the cross-currents of officially established state religions and religious persecution in Europe and come to this country filled with the hope that they could find a place in which they could pray when they pleased to the God of their faith in the language they chose.[20]   And there were men of this same faith in the power of prayer who led the fight for adoption of our Constitution and also for our Bill of Rights with the very guarantees of religious freedom that forbid the sort of governmental activity which New York has attempted here.   These men knew that the First Amendment, which tried to put an end to governmental control of religion and of prayer, was not written to destroy either.   They knew rather that it was written to quiet well-justified fears which nearly all of them felt arising out of an awareness that governments of the past had shackled men's tongues to make them speak only the religious thoughts that government wanted them to speak and to pray only to the God that government wanted them to pray to.   It is neither sacrilegious nor antireligious to say that each separate government in this country should stay out of the business of writing or sanctioning official prayers and leave that purely religious function to the people themselves and to those the people choose to look to for religious guidance.[21]

It is true that New York's establishment of its Regents' prayer as an officially approved religious doctrine of that State does not amount to a total establishment of one particular religious sect to the exclusion of all others—that, indeed, the governmental endorsement of that prayer seems relatively insignificant when compared to the governmental encroachments upon religion which were commonplace 200 years ago. To those who may subscribe to the view that because the Regents' official prayer is so brief and general there can be no danger to religious freedom in its governmental establishment, however, it may be appropriate to say in the words of James Madison, the author of the First Amendment:

> "[I]t is proper to take alarm at the first experiment on our liberties. . . . Who does not see that the same authority which can establish Christianity, in exclusion of all other Religions, may establish with the same ease any particular sect of Christians, in exclusion of all other Sects? That the same authority which can force a citizen to contribute three pence

---

[21] There is of course nothing in the decision reached here that is inconsistent with the fact that school children and others are officially encouraged to express love for our country by reciting historical documents such as the Declaration of Independence which contain references to the Deity or by singing officially espoused anthems which include the composer's professions of faith in a Supreme Being, or with the fact that there are many manifestations in our public life of belief in God. Such patriotic or ceremonial occasions bear no true resemblance to the unquestioned religious exercise that the State of New York has sponsored in this instance.

only of his property for the support of any one
establishment, may force him to conform to any other
establishment in all cases whatsoever?" [22]

The judgment of the Court of Appeals of New York
is reversed and the cause remanded for further proceedings not inconsistent with this opinion.

Reversed and remanded.

Mr. Justice Frankfurter took no part in the decision
of this case.

Mr. Justice White took no part in the consideration
or decision of this case.

---

[22] Memorial and Remonstrance against Religious Assessments, II
Writings of Madison 183, at 185–186.

Liberal Press Books are a series of topical paper-backs that deal with currently-controversial political issues, while they are still in the news. Each book is produced and published as soon as possible after the news event or political controversy to which it refers.

The purpose of the Liberal Press series is to provide the public with a more profound and searching analysis of these issues than they could obtain from the normal-length newspaper or magazine article. In many instances, this means that the entire text of key documents—judicial decisions, important speeches, Congressional debates, legislation—will be reproduced in full as part of the analysis.

The approach of the books is frankly partisan—a stand is taken and that stand is defended. But all sides of the issue are presented; and the inclusion of basic texts and source materials permits the reader to make up his own mind.